In His Own Time

A Story of family, friends And courage

Tamara Pray Frazier

ᴊulian's Legacy Publishers
Hinesville, Georgia

Manufactured in the United States of America

Second Edition

Copies may be ordered from
Julian's Legacy Publishers,
At 1-912-572-2404

ISBN: 978-0-615-22488-6

This book is dedicated to the memory of

Mr. Julian Pray (Pop)
Sunrise May 21, 1915
Sunset April 1, 2006

Mrs. Daisy Belle Pray (Mother)
Sunrise October 6, 1918
Sunset November 24, 1998

Ms. Vivian Iona Pray (Mama)
Sunrise July 1, 1943
Sunset November 17, 2003

All That I Am
All that I am and all I aspire to be
Is because of
Silenced Heroes that I call Family.
In my younger years I did not know
The wonderful, rich legacy into which I had to grow.
I am the granddaughter of Julian and Daisy
And the proud daughter of Vivian Pray-
Who not only laid the road but also
Paved the way
For me and the success I experience today…

Your Legacy Lives On…
Tammie

Table of Contents

Acknowledgements

*O*nce again I am faced with the awesome task of thanking all the wonderful people in my life that made the completion of this book possible. There are so many people who believe in me and supported this project that I could not possibly name them all, even though I tried the first time around. Instead, I will simply say thank you to my Heavenly Father for blessing me with the talent to bring Faye's story to life. You are so good to me and I am not worthy.

To my brothers and sisters, Vince, Virgil, Tamikki and Jenny- you guys have been my support system for so long. I love you! To the Pray, Frazier, and Barnard Families; all that I am is because of you. To the special families who have embraced me- the Bakers, the Thomas Family, the Jones/ King Family and the Bradwell Institute Family, thank you for supporting this project and all my endeavors. Faye and I love and appreciate you more than you will ever know.

Once again, I will acknowledge my sister-friends who always have my back. Michelle, Tammy, Lynette, Katie, Tamekia, Lisa, Stephanie, April and the Platinum 40/40's, you ladies keep me grounded. I love you all. I would also like to thank my friends, the McSalters Family at Freelance Fotographics for my new cover.

Additionally, I want to thank Mr. Jim Collins, Mr. Howe and the Graphic arts classes at Bradwell Institute for coming through for me when my back was against the wall. Thank you for your diligent work!

Extra special thanks go out to my brother Vincent and his wife, Rhonda, Renee and Michael Hemingway and my Aunt Christine... Julian's Legacy thanks you sincerely. Faye, what can I say? Thank you for making me look so good. If I had not had such a great subject, how could I possibly still write passionately about it 3 years later? Before I go any further, I would like to acknowledge my three children. Gabriele, Alex and Jordan, thank you for molding and shaping me into the productive, compassionate, patient individual that I am... I love you guys and I am proud of each of you.

And last but not least, I want to thank all the wonderful people who purchased my book, emailed, wrote letters or walked up to me on the streets and told me how much this book meant to you or someone in your life. Your blessings and prayers have been the wind beneath my wings.

Tamara Pray Frazier

Hinesville, Georgia

2008

Foreword

By Faye Baker

People frequently tell me that I am an inspiration to them and I guess it must be true because recently, I was honored to receive a "Women of Inspiration" award from the WNBA's Atlanta Dream. I stood in the company of 19 of Atlanta's most inspirational women and was presented my award by Donna Orender, who is the president of the WNBA. I was introduced by yet another inspirational woman, Lisa Borders, who is the President of the Atlanta City Council. How is that for inspirational?

Throughout the evening, I was blessed to meet some really wonderful women whose stories were different from mine but we all had one common thread; the word NO was not an option. I was in the company of an awesome group of women and though I am humbled by all the compliments, I often wonder what is it about me that is inspiring?

I am just one of many women who has experienced a life altering event. One day I was able bodied and independent and the just like that, the next day, I was fighting for my life after a horrific accident. I will not insult anyone's intelligence by trying to downplay what happened to me that day. After almost losing my life and losing my ability to walk, I was devastated.

But was I expected to just sit around and feel sorry for myself because my body became broken and I had the motor skills of a newborn baby? Was I expected to lie in bed on a daily basis and allow my family and friends to wait on me? Honestly, that was never a thought; simply because I was not raised that way and for me, giving up has never, ever been an option.

I feel like our lives are pre-destined from the time we exit our mother's wombs. God already had it planned since my existence that I would have a very traumatic experience at the age of 37. It was already in my life's blueprint that I would lose my ability to walk. But he didn't' just spring it on me. On no, He prepared me for it along the way. He gave me strong parents, supportive siblings and good friends that would be there to help me endure the most difficult time of my life.

He gave me the gift of athleticism which helped me endure the physical struggle of therapy and gave me the mind set that hard work pays off. Most importantly, He provided me with a spiritual background that gave me the strength to say "no, I do not accept the doctor's prognosis that I will never walk again" and the faith to know that through it all, He has the final say.

No, there is nothing inspirational about me. The real inspiration is God because he uses ordinary people like me to get his messages across. It is the miracles He performed *through me* that are inspirational. I do not concentrate on what has been taken away from me but rather on the things that I am still able to do. So, when adversity comes your way, always remember that as bad as it may seem, it can always be worse. When hard times threaten, you must believe in yourself. Believe that you are capable of overcoming any obstacle that is thrown in your path.

God prepares us for our battles and sometimes we do not even realize it. All we have to do is hold on to Him and we must remember if God brings you to it, He will guide you through it and that my friends, is true inspiration!

Faye Baker

Hinesville, Georgia

2008

Prologue / Fall 2004

Faith

When your heart is broken, time seems to stand still...
Your days blend with your nights and it seems
that your heart will never heal.
Though we should never question the Lord,
deep in our hearts we wonder why
But God knows what is best for you and
He hears you when you cry.
He's gently holding your hand as you walk this rocky trail.
I know he'll see you through this storm,
for my Father has yet to fail.
In this midst of these storm clouds that
seem to surround you,
Hold tight to the Master's hand and let your faith in him
see you through.
A brighter tomorrow awaits you at the end
of this long hard road.
But for today, give it all up to Him.
For, He will share your load.
                                        —T.L. Frazier

I WAS RIDING ALONG HIGHWAY 84 West in Allenhurst, Georgia. It was one of those brilliant fall days a couple of weeks before Thanksgiving when the air suddenly seems crystal clear, with the slanting sunlight at its purist. But I was not paying attention to that world. Instead I was mentally checking off the list of things that I had to do before I closed my eyes that night. As so often happened, I was feeling good and sorry for myself. I always had more to do than time to do it in, I fussed to myself. I was tired. All I wanted to do was get home and get some rest.

Having just left work for the day, I was feeling emotionally exhausted. The date was creeping up on me and I honestly didn't know how I was going to handle it. It would be my first; therefore, there was the fear of the unknown that I was dealing with. Everyone said it would probably be hard and a few friends and family members had already started handling me with kid gloves. They were trying to cover it up, but I had already anticipated their concern and though some statements and gestures were cleverly disguised, I knew exactly what they were trying to do.

As I rode along the highway, I mentally took notes as to how I would spend the rest of my afternoon. With the one-year anniversary of my mother's death looming on the horizon, my disposition had taken a dive into the negative column and my already borderline memory suffered further loss.

"This life is too hard," I told myself as I distractedly listened to an exchange between my daughter, Gabriele, and Stephanie, a co-worker who was riding with me. "I have a million and one things to do all the time," I thought. "Everyone says that I'll probably break down since I didn't do it last year," I worried. In my mind, I honestly thought that within the next two days, I was probably going to have to spend a night or two in Charter By-the-Sea, mourning my mother's death. I was nervous and worried that my children would see me lose my mind, because I wasn't going to be able to handle this setback and I fought back tears as I continued to drive.

I rounded the corner in front of the post office, I looked to my right, when at the same time my daughter said, "Look Mommy!" There, riding down the side of the highway on her three-wheeled bicycle was my friend, Faye Baker, with her brother HC walking quickly beside her. A warm, fuzzy feeling filled my heart. Blowing my horn, I raised my hand in greeting. HC waved in return, but Faye, her head bent deep in concentration, kept on peddling. I smiled as I kept riding. The thoughts that had clouded my mind just seconds before had all but disappeared.

I thought of Faye Baker peddling so diligently down the highway, and felt ashamed of myself. "How dare I complain? Then, laughing out loud, I said to myself, "She's done it again; she's made me face up to myself!""

Who is this extraordinary person who has the ability to make a grown woman chastise herself? How was it that just a glimpse of this person took my mind off of a situation that had dampened my mood for days? And most importantly, how had seeing Faye riding a bicycle enabled me to automatically find that lost strength that my mother had instilled in me from childhood? How had she taught me that *this too shall pass,* when everyone said it wouldn't without at least a "mini-breakdown?"

Well, unless you are a fan of prep basketball, the name Faye Baker may not ring a bell with you. But it should, and that's why I have written this book. With the support of friends and family I will introduce you to a formidable force of a woman who should be on everyone's who's who list of people to know. Throughout the course of this book, you will go on a journey that will introduce you to a person of remarkable strength and courage, a person who turned her own personal tragedy into a source of strength and courage for an entire community.

As you turn these pages, you will meet a woman and a group of people who stood behind, beside, and always with Faye as she made her remarkable uphill battle against terrible injuries and regained her independence. You'll understand the power of love and the strength that comes from a solid upbringing. You'll understand the importance of building friendships on solid foundations and you'll be blessed to meet a family that is truly anchored in the Lord.

In short, you will meet our hero, Faye Baker. You will learn how she dared to say no, when she was backed up against the wall of seemingly permanent paralysis. Your heart will feel her highs and lows, her strength, courage and faith.

And by the end of this story you will know that you too can do all things through Christ.

1 / Roots

*F*AYE BAKER WAS LOOKING forward to the two-hour drive to attend an anniversary celebration at the Mount Zion AME church in Round O, South Carolina. After all, she had been working overtime at her job as head coach of the Bradwell Institute "Lady Tigers" basketball team. Of late, the perennial conference champs had been practicing extra hard and Faye was feeling the stress. Time off for the excursion to Round O, she felt, might be just what the doctor ordered, Especially since she wasn't the one doing the driving.

"Faye, why don't we ride in your truck?" her mother had suggested with an innocent smile. Glancing over at her mother, Faye just shook her head. Ethel Baker had her own innocent way of letting Faye know what she wanted her to do without actually having to tell her. "There's going to be a lot of people on the church van."

"I know what she's up to," Faye thought. "I'm not falling for it this time. Like always, I'll end up driving there and back."

This time Faye didn't take her up on her suggestion. "I need to relax, Mother. I really don't feel like driving," Faye had said "Maybe I'll take a snooze while we're on the way. I'm so tired, I'll be asleep before we get out of Hinesville."

Then, smiling at the thought of the festivities ahead, she added, "There's going to be plenty of foot-stomping and hand clapping to wake me up when we get there, not to mention the food. Those ladies can really throw down in the kitchen."

❧

The youngest of five children born to Henry and Ethel Baker, Faye was raised in Allenhurst, Ga., population 750, one of many rural Georgia communities scattered through the rich farmlands of the coastal plain. Allenhurst boasted one small convenience store with a door that led to the local post office. The same postal clerk had passed out mail for generations and knew every resident by name.

Indeed, everyone knew everyone else. It was the proverbial village, in which families helped to raise each other's children. If you saw someone else's child misbehaving in public, it was not only acceptable, but even expected, that you should "get a switch and tan their hides."

There were no traffic lights, recreation centers, parks or restaurants that catered to children. Nevertheless, the Baker children—Faye, her older sister, Barbara and older brothers, Henry Jr. (HC), Ronald, and Derrell—never lacked something to do. Whether they were playing in the nearby woods, competing in some made up game or simply playing marbles in the yard, they were always busy. By the time Faye was in elementary school and integration became a reality, they were able to participate in organized sports activities in the nearby city of Hinesville at the Liberty County Recreation Department.

The "Rec," (as it was called), was run by Mr. Charles Shuman, and its athletic programs produced some of the greatest athletes that Hinesville has ever seen. Mr. Shuman took a personal interest in each of his participants and made it his business to get to know their families. It is said that he could look at a newcomer and instinctively know what family they came from.

"Oh, she runs just like a Pray," or "He must be related to the Bakers, hitting the ball like that," are things he might be heard to say.

As a young girl, Faye often tagged along behind her older brothers when they went to the Rec, participated in whatever sports were in season, and took part in whatever activities her church had going on at the time. But for the most part, athletics took up a large portion of their time. "My brothers and sister were great athletes, Faye remembered. "Keeping up with them made me one very tough little girl."

"From the very beginning," Faye remembers, "I hated to lose. I played hard, and I played to win." It was in the heart of her family that she developed the don't-give-up, never-say-die attitude that she carries with her to this day. "My brother Derrell," she recalls, "though four years my senior was closest to me in age, so he was always the one I measured myself against. I was always trying to do the things that I saw him do."

Derrell Baker excelled in every sport in high school and actually signed a football scholarship to play with East Carolina University. He later changed his mind and signed with a junior college to pursue his first love, baseball.

Barbara Baker was a standout in basketball throughout high school. Ronald and Henry Jr. (HC) both excelled in football, baseball and basketball in high school. Two of Faye's brothers went on to play professional baseball in the minor leagues. HC played for the Boston Red Sox organization and Derrell for that of the Montreal Expos. So it was natural for Faye to follow suit and eventually take up coaching and teaching as a career.

"My brothers and sister provided models for me to follow," Faye explains. "When the chips were down and I had to survive or die, walk or be confined to a wheelchair for life, it was from them that I drew the great, hard-headed strength and determination that would be necessary for my recovery."

In her teen-age years, Faye spent most of her summers in Chicago with her older sister, Barbara. Barbara and her husband, Michael (Mickey) Derrick, were the parents of two boys, so they loved having a girl in the house. "I learned a lot from her," Faye remembers. "She spent a lot of time teaching me to be confidant and self-reliant. I am grateful to her for helping instill in me a spirit of independence."

But it was her parents that Faye credits with raising her to become the strong, determined person that she is. "Mother and Daddy somehow found a recipe that balanced the proper dosage of love with just the right amount of discipline," Faye says. "We were surrounded by love and we were always made to feel valued and cherished, but there was never a problem with them administering punishment when one of us needed it."

The word of God was first and foremost in the Baker household. Faye's parents made sure that all their children were exposed to the Bible at a young age. "Not only did they teach us about it," Faye affirms. "They led by example. They always *showed* us the right way. That's the best teaching of all, and I have always tried to follow them in this in my own teaching. As adults, the decisions we make are our own to make, but believe me, the lessons that I learned from my parents are right here with me, guiding me everyday. Its no accident," she adds, "that I am strong in faith, as well as mind, body and spirit."

"I was raised to believe that everything happens for a reason. God doesn't make any mistakes, so when I was chosen it was not by accident. Most importantly, I know that I am a part of a divine plan, and I must say that I am amazed that he thought enough of me to use me. I would not have knowingly chosen this route for myself, but God chose it for me, so I have no problem being his vessel. Hopefully, my story will inspire at least one person. If so, then my job is done."

2 / Out of the Blue

*B*UT ON THIS DAY, October 22, 2000, Faye was taking it easy, napping on the third seat of the church van heading for the dedication at Round O. The nap would not last long. The last thing Faye remembered before losing consciousness was a noise like that of an explosion. The back left tire of the the white Ford van had blown out, and it was shaking violently as it swerved back and forth across Interstate 95. Its thirteen occupants were screaming and crying out because they all knew that a crash was imminent. Inspite of Oeraetta's frantic efforts to control the van, it hit the shoulder of the highway, rolling over three times before coming to a rocky halt upside down in the ditch.

"Faye, brace yourself," Michelle had shouted as she put her knees on the back of the seat ahead of her. Disoriented and still groggy from sleep, Faye had only milliseconds to react before the van went into its tailspin. As the vehicle settled in its upside down position, those inside were screaming and trying to find a way out, but Faye lay immobile. As darkness engulfed her, she was oblivious to the chaos that was taking place around her.

Faye! Faye! Are you all right?" Michelle asked frantically. Shaking Faye's shoulder, Michelle looked helplessly around for some help. The sight of her roommate lying in an awkward position as everyone else tried to escape the wreckage had alarmed Michelle, but her medical training had taught her to remain calm during crisis situations. But this wasn't any normal crisis situation. None of the prior situations she had dealt with had ever involved someone close to her. She was trying to keep her composure, but she was about one second away from panic. "Calm down, girl," Michelle slowly cautioned herself just as she heard a moan escape Faye's lips and her eyes fluttered open.

Looking at the blurred form of her roommate, Faye repeatedly blinked her eyes until Michelle's face came into focus. Taking in the broken windows, the smoke, noise and confusion, she realized that something was terribly wrong. "OK Faye" she prodded herself, " you have to get up."

Her mind was telegraphing her body to get out of the wrecked van, but her body was not responding. In her half-conscious state, this puzzled her. "Why am I not moving," she wondered. No matter how desperately she tried to do so, she could not move any part of her body. Her legs lay still and crooked on the floor. Coughing from the dust, Faye had the urge to cover her mouth, but her arms refused to move like she wanted them to. Instead of moving they were slightly jerking and her legs felt like they were floating in space. She was experiencing a weird, kind of weightless feeling. A feeling that conjured up horrible images in her mind. A stricken look came to Faye's eyes as the magnitude of the situation became clear.

"Michelle," she cried out in panic "I can't feel my legs. You have to help me get up," she shouted. The windows in the van were shattered and the doors jammed. Other members of the church had surrounded the wreck and were trying to help the uninjured passengers out to safety. As the other riders clambered pass her to crawl out of the back window of the van, a sense of unease settled in the pit of Michelle's stomach. "Hold on, Faye. I'm going to help them get off," Michelle yelled over her shoulder. "I'll be back," she added as she disappeared through the window.

Faye's eyes fell on the last retreating back. Seventeen-year-old Teddrick Brown was the lone teenager in the group. A few minutes prior to the crash he and his younger brothers were sharing the Sunday edition of their local newspaper, *The Coastal Courier*. Teddy (as he is known to family and friends) had been excelling in football at Bradwell Institute, and it seemed he was featured in the sports pages of all of the latest issues.

"Look, there's your name again, Teddy," Rishad Grigsby had said just seconds before the crash.

⁂

"Come on Kijuan, let me get you through this window," Teddy shouted as he reached for his youngest brother and boosted him up to the side window.

Moments before he was a carefree teenager with grades and football stats on his mind, and in the next instant—in the absence of his parents—he was left with the sole responsibility of making sure his younger brothers, Keddrick and Kijuan and their friend Rishad, were safe.

Now he felt something tugging on his ankle. Looking down, Teddy saw a dusty arm slightly jerking back and forth near his foot. Looking to see whose arm it was, Teddy looked into the pleading eyes of his former Sunday school teacher.

"Please don't leave me in this van, Teddy. Please don't leave me," Faye pleaded as Teddrick was lifting Rishad out of the window. He saw Coach Baker lying there with her arm swinging and immediately knew that there was something wrong with her.

"As soon as I make sure that my brothers are safe, I'll be back. Come on Keddrick!" he shouted as he grabbed his brother (who was scrambling around trying to locate his pair of beloved drum sticks) and pushed him out the side window.

Meanwhile, Michelle had returned. "Faye, Faye, I'm back," Michelle said as she climbed back into the window. Crawling quickly through the dust to her roommate and positioning herself behind Faye's head Michelle said, "OK, Faye, I'm going to try to pull you and get you out." Putting her forearms under Faye's armpits she took a deep breath and pulled as hard as she could, but to no avail. "She's too heavy," Michelle thought. Tears of frustration appeared in the corners of her light brown eyes as she realized that she was not going to be able to help Faye. Not ready to give up, she pulled again with all of the strength her 120-pound body could muster, but still Faye remained in the same spot. She pulled so hard that her feet began to slip on the gritty surface. Sliding down on the dusty van floor behind her roommate, Michelle tried desperately not to cry. Smoke had begun to fill the van and Michelle coughed out loud from the thick clouds of dust and smoke that surrounded them. "Somebody is going to come and help us, Faye," Michelle said trying to reassure her roommate as she silently prayed that she was right.

Feeling helpless and afraid were not emotions that Faye Baker was used to. A tall, solidly built woman with a commanding presence, Faye was used to being the "go to" person when help was needed, but today she was the one who needed help. Along with Faye and Michelle, one teenager, three small children, five older women, and a middle-aged, married couple, had been in the van. Amazingly enough, every one of them had been able to safely get off the van. Faye was the sole exception. As she lay in the upside down van, her thoughts turned to her mother. Was she hurt? Where was she? Faye knew one thing for sure: wherever Ethel Baker was, she was worried about her child.

"Michelle, I want you to go find Mother and see if she is alright," Faye said "Let her know that I'm OK," she added. Not wanting to leave her friend's side, Michelle tried to argue, but was cut off by Faye's insistent voice.

"No Michelle, go and check on her for me. I'll be all right. Let me know if she's OK." Reluctantly Michelle crawled out of the back window to do Faye's bidding just as Teddy was climbing back in the window.

Lying immobile in the wrecked van, Faye knew that she must have suffered a very serious injury, but at the moment the only thing on her mind was getting out of the van. Would it catch on fire? Would she be left to burn to death? Was her mother all right? She felt as though she were looking death in the face, and this scared her more than anything. Sweat beaded on her forehead and her heartbeat pounded away a mile a minute. Time seemed to stand still as Faye anxiously waited for Michelle to return with news concerning her mother. Her eyes were darting nervously from one corner of the van to the other when they came to rest on the one thing that she feared the most, leaking fluids. As Faye's breathing became short and ragged, she shouted with every ounce of energy that she had left in her body.

"Teddy, Help!" *Oh my God, this van is going to blow up with me on it*, she thought as her heartbeat accelerated. Lord, please don't let this van blow up," she chanted over and over inside her head. "I am not ready to die. I can't die yet," she prayed.

"Teddy, look!" Faye shouted as she looked in the direction of the fluids running down the side of the van. "You have to help me get out. We have to hurry Teddy. The van might blow up," she called out.

Panicked from the frightening tone of Faye's voice, Teddy jumped. As he prepared himself to try to drag Faye, his progress was halted by what can only be described as an angel in disguise, Sister Cheryl Robinson.

"Don't move her, Teddy! She called out as she poked her head in the back window. "She can't be moved. Just let her stay still until the paramedics get here."

Having worked as a triage nurse, Sister Robinson knew the danger of moving a person who might have spinal cord injuries. Moving her could have further damaged her spinal cord, which would have compromised breathing hence, causing respiratory distress.

"But the fluids are running down the side," he protested.

"We can't, Teddy. Just sit tight. They're almost here," Sister Cheryl answered. Extremely handsome and mature beyond his years, Teddrick Brown sat back down beside Coach Baker on the dusty van silently praying until the paramedics arrived. Then and only then did he move from her side.

3 / The Golden Hour

*A*S SIRENS WHIRRED in the distance, Mrs. Ethel Baker lay on the grassy bank of the highway. Lying flat on the ground, tears streamed down her face. The memory of swerving and flipping continued to play over and over in her mind like a bad movie, and her body heaved with tears. Her front passenger seat had afforded an unobstructed view of the highway as they flipped head over heels. Her heartbeat quickened and she continued to cry uncontrollably. She remembered lying on her side in pain from cuts suffered when someone had come and helped her off the van through shattered glass. Yet, as blood seeped from the cut on her left ankle, Ethel barely acknowledged the pain. She was beside herself with worry for her youngest child.

"Where is Faye, she wondered?" Lifting herself up on her elbows, she felt a stab of pain, but she was determined to look and see if she could locate Faye. She did not like the fact that Faye was not up on the highway.

"I knew something must have been wrong with Faye because if she were well, she would've been by my side; making sure I was all right," she would later say. Lifting her head, she spied Michelle coming in her direction. "Michelle," she shouted, "where's Faye? Is she all right?"

"Faye's all right, Mrs. Baker," Michelle had replied somewhat distractedly. "She sent me to check on you. Are you OK?"

"I just have this cut, but I am worried about Faye."

Not wanting to alarm Ethel, Michelle replied, "They're helping her now. She'll be up here soon."

Pacing the shoulder of the highway, Michelle had tried to reassure everyone that Faye was conscious and doing OK despite not being able to move her legs. Reaching into the pocket of her dusty, black slacks, Michelle retrieved Faye's cell phone that she had picked up in the van, trying to figure out who she should call.

"Henry, where are you? Why is it taking the other van so long to get here?" Ethel Baker asked over and over again to anyone who would listen. Sighing in frustration, Ethel made up her mind to do the only thing she could do. She prayed. She knew if she let go and let Him handle the situation, He would not let her down. Looking around, she knew that things could've been much worse, but God was handling things. Had he not seen to it that everyone emerged from this wreck alive? That was the first blessing. Having a nurse on hand had also helped the situation. Shuddering at the thought of what could've been, Ethel wiped at her tears and continued to lay and pray.

Having grown up in a God-fearing household and having raised her family to believe in His word, Mrs. Ethel knew that God *never* closes a door without opening up a window. She prayed with all of her heart that her baby would be fine. It was hard not giving into the grief that she was feeling, but she was trying with all her might to "let go and let God."

The problem was that no one was telling her anything, so naturally all sorts of thoughts went through her head. The ambulance pulled up and the paramedics rushed past her to the ditch, which only confirmed what she already suspected. Faye was really hurt. "Oh Lord, please take care of my baby," she cried out over and over again. So constant were her pleas that a stranger walked over, telling her in a voice tinged with annoyance "Lady, your friend is going to be all right!"

"That's not my friend, that's my baby," Ethel shouted back equally annoyed, as she continued her vigilant prayer.

As traffic in the northbound lane of I-95 came to a complete and total halt, emergency workers worked diligently to remove Faye Baker from the wreckage. People not involved in the accident got out of their cars and stood alongside the victims of the wreck. As the state troopers tried to keep the situation under control, the traffic continued to back up for hours.

Down in the van, the response team carefully cut from her body the black dress that Faye had picked out for Camp Meeting. Fearing the worse, they painstakingly mobilized her head with a neck brace. Listening closely for any information, Teddy stood by waiting to hear anything he could about Faye's condition. He thought about the Coach Baker that he knew. She was one of the first persons to teach him about the Bible. He had known Faye since he was in elementary school. She had been his Sunday School teacher and then a teacher at his school. He often saw her at school, and she always made a point of asking about his grades and athletic performances. Seeing her like this scared him because she had always been so strong and able-bodied. Pacing back and forth, he thanked God for keeping him safe and he prayed that Faye would be all right.

Emergency response workers were preparing to transport Faye to Memorial Medical Center by Lifestar helicopter. Six other passengers would later be treated for minor injuries and taken to nearby hospitals in the Hardeeville area, but aside from Faye, no one was seriously injured.

4 / A Test of Faith

*T*HE PARAMEDICS WERE hard at work trying to stabilize Faye and make her transport-ready when the van carrying her father, Reverend Lee and the families of the other passengers arrived.

Surveying the damage and destruction that lay in front of him, Reverend Stephen Lee just knew that when the smoke cleared he was going to find that at least one member of his flock had perished in the accident. He had been riding about a mile and a half ahead of the other van when one of the members who was driving a private car raced up beside their van and communicated that there had been an accident. The car immediately turned around on the median but the van continued on to the next exit.

Seeing the car turn on the median was an immediate sign of trouble. Why else would they break the law and risk getting a ticket if it wasn't an emergency? Mr. John Henderson was the driver of this van and upon learning there had been an accident, he began to panic. His wife, Oraetta was driving the van with the ladies and the kids and the thought of her being involved in an accident had him shaken up. His driving became increasingly erratic as they made their way back. Seeing how visibly upset he was, Reverend Lee spoke to him gently.

"Brother Henderson, please pull over to the side," Reverend Lee said. "You're too upset to drive" As the van came to a halt, Teddrick's father, Wilson, got up out of his seat. "I'll take over," he said as he traded places with John.

Sitting in the back of the van, Gloria Brown's mind immediately went back to the church parking lot. She remembered her unease at not having a seat in the van with her boys. "I knew it," she thought. "I felt it," she murmured as tears came to her eyes and a tortured moan escaped from her lips. "My boys", she mumbled. "My boys."

As they pulled over in the southbound lane, Reverend Lee could not believe the sight that awaited them. He would later say the first thing that came to his mind was "Lord, what have I done to deserve this?"

Stephen Lee had been leading the Bethel AME church family for approximately five months on that fateful day in October. As a matter of fact, this was his first pastorate, and for the life of him, he could not understand something of this magnitude occurring so soon into his tenure. But for the time being he had to concentrate on administering to his people in their time of need.

As he got out of his own van, he gazed at the flashing lights of the EMS vehicles, as though mesmerized. Then, inhaling deeply and murmuring a short prayer for strength, he began to scan the faces so he could account for his church members. "OK," he reminded himself, "there were thirteen people in the van." Looking across the median he could see Sister Pauline (Travis) check, Sister Beverly (Pitts), check, Sister Jeannette (Pray) is over there," he stated as he continued to check his members off. Looking to the left he could see Sister Ethel (Baker) lying on the bank and Sister Oeretta (Henderson) who had been driving the van.

"That's five," he said as he continued to search. "There are the Johnsons. They make seven. One, two, three boys" he said as he included Rishad, Keddrick and Kijuan, who were slightly out of sight sitting on the hill embracing each other. "They make ten." Glancing to his left, he saw Michelle pacing the bank. "That makes eleven.

Standing beside Mr. Henry Baker, he soon realized that Faye was missing. And as he turned to comfort Mr. Baker he heard the tortured cry of Gloria Brown. " Aaah!" she screamed. "Oh Lord, where are my boys?" she shouted as she made a move to cross the highway. Seeing that she was focused solely on finding her children and not the traffic in the southbound lane that continued to whiz by, Reverend Lee, along with Gloria's husband and another church member, held her back until it was safe to cross. As they crossed the median, he could see the overturned van in the ditch where EMS workers were going back and forth making trips to and from their van.

Keddrick and Kijuan Brown had been sitting on the grassy hill waiting for their older brother, Teddy. He had helped them get out of the van before running back to help Faye. As they sat on the grassy hill beside their good friend, Rishad, they all cried. The young boys were both frightened and shaken up from the accident and they all wished Teddy would come from down in the ditch. Looking up they noticed their parents running towards them, and they immediately felt safer. Gloria was so overcome with relief; all she could do was cry. Looking around, though, she didn't see Teddy anywhere. "Where is my baby," she wondered. "Oh heavenly father, where is my son," she started to pray. As she rocked back and forth with her arms around the distraught boys, she cried and prayed alternately.

"Teddy must be in that van and he must be hurt," she thought. "That must be why no one is saying anything to me. Lord, I don't want you to think I am not grateful, or that I'm being greedy, but Lord, I need Teddy too. Lord, I thank you for keeping these two safe," she sniffed, "but I need my baby!" She prayed as she cried with all the grief of a mother who had lost her child.

With all of the chaos going on, no one thought to tell Gloria that Teddrick was alive and well, watching over his former Sunday school teacher in her time of need.

About twenty yards away, Henry Baker heard his wife's pleas and rushed to where she lay. Looking up, she cried out, "Henry, Faye is still in that van. I don't know if she's hurt! She must be..." her voice trailed off as Henry interrupted her. "I'll go and check, but are you all right?" he asked, glancing at Ethel's bloody leg and tear-streaked face.

"Henry, I'm all right. Find out about Faye," she wailed. But before Henry could make a move, a disturbance down in the ditch caused him to stop.

Teddy was the first to arrive at the top of the hill, prompting Gloria Brown to shout out a heartfelt "Thank you, Lord!" while continuing to cry. God had spared her children's lives and she was grateful, but then she noticed that someone was still in the van. "Lord, someone is still in there" she cried while hugging all three of her boys as she continued to cry for her church member who was still trapped in the van.

Joining hands, the Bethel AME church family solemnly bowed their heads and said a prayer. As the prayer came near a close, a gurney carrying Faye came into view and time stood still for several people. Ethel Baker lay helplessly with her hands covering her mouth, muffling her cries. Henry Baker became paralyzed with fear. Seeing his youngest daughter lying so still on the gurney with her eyes closed shocked him. As the seriousness of the situation hit him, he quickly fell into step beside the gurney.

"This is my daughter," he stammered. "Is she all right?" he asked. "

Sir the patient is critical," the EMT worker replied, as they continued to push the gurney toward the waiting Lifestar.

"I need to go with her," Henry said, his eyes pleading with the technician.

"Sorry Sir. You have to step to the side. No one can go in the helicopter," the tech replied as they arrived beside it.

Totally devastated and more frightened than he had ever been before, Mr. Baker ran back to his wife's side. Another ambulance had arrived and an EMT was preparing Mrs. Baker for transport. Not wanting to worry his wife, Henry kept the conversation steered away from Faye.

"Can I ride in the ambulance with her?" he asked.

"No sir, I'm sorry, but there's no room," she said as they wheeled Mrs. Ethel to the waiting ambulance. Glancing around helplessly, Mr. Baker looked for someone, anyone, to share his grief with. Spying Michelle, he quickly closed the distance between the two of them.

5 / Help Is On the Way

MICHELLE, CALL HC. Tell him he needs to come here, now!" Mr. Baker shouted with urgency.

"I don't know the number. Do you know the number?" Michelle cried. Of all times for his mind to fail him, when he really needed to remember, Henry's mind drew a complete blank. He could not think of his son's number if his life depended on it. As a matter of fact, he would not have been able to remember his own number at that time. "Give me the phone," he said reaching out his hand. "Lord, please help me remember this number." Henry prayed as he glanced down the highway, spying Reverend Lee's retreating back. "Where is he going?" he wondered as his fingers dialed the phone, and it began to ring in the HC Baker household.

As he walked quickly down the highway, Reverend Lee swiped at the tears that had suddenly sprung to his eyes. Seeing Faye lying so still on the gurney had scared the life out of him and he felt like he needed a few minutes to himself. "She's lying so still . . . I wonder if she's . . . ."

His mind refused to let his mouth voice the thoughts that rushed through his head. This accident was taking a toll on him, and he didn't want anyone to see him in this condition. As each tear rolled down his cheek, he swiftly wiped it away, chastising himself the entire time. "You are a leader," he said to himself. "You have to hold it together." Taking a deep breath, he dried the last of his tears before he turned to walk the thirty yards back to the accident scene.

As he turned, his eyes fell upon a carload of teenage boys in the southbound lane. "Slow down, man" one of the boys told the driver. "I can't see." The boys were hanging out the window, gawking and the one young man who was doing the talking had his eyes firmly glued to a video camera, filming the entire scene as they passed by. Anger and disgust rose inside him. "At that moment, I didn't feel very Reverend-like" Stephen would later admit. "I just felt like plain old Steve. I was angry, scared and completely lost, and it both-ered me so much that one person's pain was being used for another's recreation. Not one of the classes that I took in seminary prepared me for anything like this. I was totally lost, and, as a pastor, I felt completely useless."

As he stood along the highway, Reverend Lee thought back to earlier that day when they were in the church park-ing lot; how he had assembled the members who were riding on his van; how they had joined hands and said a prayer for a safe journey. Breaking into a cold sweat he realized that he had not said a prayer with the other van. Was this his fault, he wondered? Was he somehow to blame for what had happened? A feeling of foreboding settled in the pit of his stomach, and his breath started coming in short gasps. Guilt and despair washed over him, as his mind played an omi-nous tune that seemed to be saying, "You failed them, you failed them."

Reeling from his revelation, his heart began to beat a staccato rhythm that he was sure could be heard over the helicopter's propellers as it took off for the hospital. Reverend Lee closed his eyes and quickly began to pray for strength. And you can imagine his relief to turn and find himself staring into the kindly, concerned eyes of Cheryl Robinson.

"Reverend Lee, are you all right?" she asked while gently rubbing her hand up and down his back.

Looking heavenward he replied, "Soon, Sister. Soon I will be," as he sent up a silent message of thanks for her presence. In the back of his mind, he kept repeating a mantra over and over, "I can do all things through Christ, which strengthens me"

Shortly after the last ambulance left, Faye's eldest brother, HC, arrived at the accident scene. Arriving with his youngest daughter, Chandra in tow, HC attempted to get as much information as possible before loading up his father and his Aunt Pauline and setting out for the hospital in Hilton Head where they had taken his mother.

Meanwhile, back in Hinesville, the telephone in Tamara Frazier's household was ringing.

6 / A Friend In Need

$\mathcal{M}$OMMY, MICHELLE WANTS you on the phone" was the greeting that met Tamara Frazier as she entered the front door of her apartment. Taking the cordless phone from her daughter Gabriele's hand, Tamara looked at her in frustration. "You could at least help me with the bags," she said as she struggled to put down the grocery bags that she was carrying. Grabbing two bags, Gabriele rushed off to the kitchen as her mother took the phone call.

"What's up, Shelle?" she breathed into the receiver

"Tamara, we've been in an accident," Michelle cried. "Faye's hurt. I think she's paralyzed" she rushed on.

"Wait! Hold on a minute." Tamara interrupted. "What are you talking about, Shelle? Start from the beginning." As she said this she noticed that her shouting had startled her mother, who had been dozing on the sofa. "Oops, sorry Mama," she whispered.

Michelle tried to compose herself on the other end of the line. Wiping her tears with the back of her hand, she tried to explain what had taken place. "We were just riding on I-95 going to church, and we heard a loud noise because the tire blew out. The van started swerving back and forth, and Faye was asleep. We flipped over three times, and now

Faye can't feel her legs. I think she's paralyzed," she continued on in a muffled whisper. As her last bit of composure disappeared, she broke down and began sobbing.

Hearing her friend cry alarmed Tamara. She knew immediately that this accident was serious because Michelle rarely cried. Even when things were as bad as they could get, she could always manage to shrug her shoulders and giggle away her troubles.   .

"Michelle, where are you? Do you want me to come and get you?" Tamara asked. "We are on 95, right before the exit to your job. . . . Yes, I do need you to come and get me, please." She tearfully responded. "Oh, and Tamara," she paused before going on, "it might be hard for you to get to me because traffic is backed up. They landed a Lifestar helicopter in the middle of the highway. They took Faye to Memorial in Savannah. HC just got here. He said he had to ride on the shoulder of the road to get here. Bring me something to put on, too. My clothes are ruined," she said, fatigue showing in her voice.

"I'm coming right now, Shelle," Tamara responded before running to the staircase. Taking the stairs two at a time, Tamara ran into her bedroom where she pillaged through her dresser drawers until she found a pair of black sweat pants and a hooded sweatshirt. Bounding down the stairs she shouted to her mother, Vivian. "Mama, Michelle and Faye were in an accident. Michelle says Faye might be paralyzed. They landed a Lifestar in the middle of I-95. It must be bad. Gotta go to Savannah. I'll call you," she yelled as she slammed the front door, leaving Vivian stunned and confused.

Riding along Highway 17 in Richmond Hill, Tamara decided to take a detour and stop by Memorial Medical Center before going to pick up Michelle. "I'll just check on Faye's condition," she thought. "Maybe I'll have some good news by the time I see Michelle. Perhaps it's not as bad as it looks," she told herself. "But a Lifestar? I don't know. I mean, they didn't use a helicopter when Kaye had his accident last year." She had begun to speak out loud.

As she drove the familiar path to Memorial hospital, Tamara's mind drifted back to the previous year when her then boyfriend was involved in a head-on collision during one of the worst flooding seasons that Hinesville and Savannah had ever witnessed. "Kaye almost died in that accident and the other driver did die," she continued to debate with herself. "But, they still didn't use Lifestar." She stepped harder on the gas pedal as she made the left turn onto the Southwest Bypass that would take her directly to the hospital.

❧

After picking up Mrs. Baker, HC and the whole Baker clan set out for Savannah. Everyone seemed to be in his or her own little world. In the silence, HC's cell phone suddenly rang, bringing everyone to attention.

"Hello" he answered. It was Belle, HC's wife of almost 23 years. Silence followed as he listened intently to his wife recount the doctor's prognosis. "Yes, OK," was the only thing anyone in the cab of the truck heard as HC hung up the phone a short while later.

"Bubba, what did they say?" asked Mrs. Ethel, using her son's childhood nickname. Holding her breath while waiting for a response, Mrs. Ethel let out a long sigh when he answered.

"Mother, don't worry. Belle said Faye is going to be OK."

A chorus of "Thank Gods" and "Thank you, Lords" could be heard throughout the truck even as a feeling of unease settled around HC while he continued on his journey to Memorial Medical Center. Inside he was in turmoil. He was hurting for the baby sister who was going through this nightmare and also hurting because the news that he had reported to his parents was in fact the opposite of what his wife had said. According to Belle, the prognosis was not good. The doctors were saying that his baby sister was going to be anything but OK.

After hanging up the phone with her husband, Lily Baker (Belle, as she's known to family and friends) sat staring at the white-tiled hallway, deep in thought about what the doctors had just told her about her sister-in-law. As her mind wandered, a hand aroused her with a light tap on the shoulder. When she looked up there were four people standing in front of her. Relief washed over her because now she had someone here to support her.

Tamara had been the next person to arrive at the emergency room. She had just located Lily when Michelle burst through the emergency room door with Mr. and Mrs. Sandy

Williams following closely behind. They had barely ex-changed greetings with Lily when two emergency room doc-tors approached them.

"If we have more family present, we can update you on the patient's condition," one of the doctors said. As every-one slowly walked to the family conference room at the end of the hallway, an ominous feeling hung in the air. It was as if everyone present were bearing the weight of the world.

"Well, I think everyone should take a seat," he suggested. As everyone shuffled around to find a chair the other doctor began. "Ms. Baker has suffered an injury at the Cervical 6/7 vertebrae"

As everyone looked around with confusion written on their faces, the doctor was interrupted with, "Excuse me, doctor, but can you please put that in terms that we can understand?"

This came from Lily, who was waging her own battle with her emotions.

"Well, as you wish," he said looking into Lily's tortured brown eyes. "Miss Baker has broken her neck and her spine is crushed. She is paralyzed and she is never going to walk again," he said with finality. It was said with such finality that it took everyone by surprise.

Despite the fact that everyone knew the accident was serious, they were all holding out for a miracle, but this doc-tor was unable to deliver. As a matter of fact, he left no room for an eventual recovery. He did not say, "There's a chance that she may walk again." He said unequivocally that she would never walk again.

We were devastated. "Dr. are you a Christian? Do you

believe in God?" Belle asked while staring the doctor in the eyes. Lifting her left eyebrow, she waited for an answer.

The question surprised the doctor because a short while earlier, this same woman had been completely distraught. Hearing the doctor's prognosis had ignited a spark of anger in Belle, but mostly she was taken aback by his callousness.

"How does he know what she *won't* do?" she thought. "He's not God."

Recognizing that she was letting her emotions get the best of her, Belle chastised herself and continued to listen to the doctor. It was not her intent to get angry with these people, but they were talking about her sister-in-law. She was very fond of Faye and so were her two teenage daughters. Faye had often taken up the slack with Genese and Chandra. They loved their aunt Faye to death. Belle was not going to let anyone speak any negativity into this situation!

Caught off guard, the doctor stammered out, "Well, yes. Yes, I am a Christian." To which Belle replied, "Then you will understand when I tell you that we aren't going to claim that. We are only going to claim a healing," putting emphasis on the word "healing."

The doctor was momentarily speechless. Then he recovered and proceeded with the rest of his statement. He informed the group that Faye was scheduled for a procedure called spinal fusion surgery that would be done the next day. This surgery is designed to repair the broken bones in the neck. "Is this surgery going to help her walk again?" a voice asked. "No," the doctor replied. As he glanced around he continued on "This surgery will only prevent her from having to wear a halo. You may have seen one on the actor Christopher Reeve. He wears a halo," he said as he made a circle with his hands to demonstrate where the halo would fit the head." This surgery is not going to do anything to help her spine," he concluded. Surveying the room, one person seemed unaffected by the doctor's proclamation, Lily Belle Baker. She was silently thinking how quickly things change. In the blink of an eye, her family's life had been altered.

7 / Claim It!

*L*ILY BAKER HAD BEEN riding along Highway 84 in Waycross, Georgia, returning from a homecoming celebration at her alma mater, Fort Valley State, when she received a phone call from her husband. HC informed her that he was on his way to South Carolina to pick up his parents because there had been an accident and Faye had been hurt. She was being airlifted to Memorial Medical Center in Savannah, but the extent of her injuries was still unknown.

Immediately after dropping her sister off at her home in Jesup, Lily made a beeline for Savannah. As she passed through Allenhurst, Lily glanced over at her in-law's home, quietly nestled in a private spot off the highway. She thought about the family that she had become a part of twenty-three years earlier. What would a death do to them? "Lord, I can't think any bad thoughts," she thought as she sped through Hinesville without one thought of being stopped by the police.

Reaching the hospital, she discovered that she was the lone member of the Baker family to have arrived. The emergency room physician met with her to discuss Faye's condition.

"I was shaking when the doctors came to speak with me about Faye's condition," Lily remembers. "He said that she had sustained damage to her spinal cord and that she wasn't going to walk again."

Immediately, Lily felt sick to her stomach as tears came to her eyes and began rolling down her cheeks. "This can't be happening. This cannot be happening," she thought as she listened to the doctor.

Having walked into this situation totally uninformed, she was nothing less than stunned. "Mrs. Baker, can we call someone for you?" the physician had asked. "No thank-you," she answered after a short time.

Drying her eyes, Lily tried to gather herself. "I have to think positive," she told herself.

"Just stop for a minute, Belle," she cautioned herself. "You are the only one here with Faye. She needs you to be positive," she had to keep telling herself over and over again. For a minute she stood up in the corridor and prayed like she had never prayed before, then she went to phone her husband.

"HC," she said when he picked up the phone. "Listen very carefully to what I'm telling you. The doctors say that Faye is paralyzed and that she won't be able to walk again. But listen to me while I have you on the phone. I want us together to claim a recovery," she said. "Do you believe that she can get better?"

"Yes" was the response she received from her husband, but his voice betrayed his doubt and hesitation

"No, I want to hear it in your voice. I want you to claim it. We aren't going to accept anything less than a recovery. Now, I have to go. I'll see you when you get here,"

8 / The Nightmare

*U*PON HER ARRIVAL AT Memorial hospital, Faye was catheterized, given steroids and administered an IV. It is believed that these procedures give trauma victims a better chance at recovery if given within the first two hours after the injury occurs. The steroids are used to reduce the swelling around the spinal cord and the fluids help control the blood pressure.

The next step for Faye was a battery of tests: MRI, CT scan, X-rays, and pinprick tests. At first observation by the paramedics, her injury was said to be a *complete injury*, which means that the spine was completely severed. The X-rays would later reveal that the spinal cord was not severed, but crushed, and that there was injury to the Cervical 6/7 vertebrae. When administered, the pinprick sensation tests showed that Faye had no feeling below the point of injury. In other words, this active, lively, athletic, basketball coach had suffered a broken neck and was paralyzed from the waist down.

❧

As Dr. Horne entered the hospital room, Faye lay on the hospital bed lost in thought. On her face she wore a puzzled frown. How had she gotten here? She was having an extremely difficult time remembering what events had led up to her lying here not being able to feel her legs. All she could remember was waking up in the emergency room with lots of people swirling around her, speaking in urgent tones. Later she would recall some parts of the accident, but for now she only knew that she had suffered a serious injury.

As Dr. Horne came to stand over Faye, her eyes went immediately to his.

"Well, Miss Baker, things don't look too good for you," he started. "First off, you've suffered damage to the cervical 6/7 vertebrae. In layman's terms you've broken your neck. You've also crushed your spine" He hastened to add, "Although your cord is not completely severed, it has sustained severe damage." Hesitating, he added, "You may never walk again."

Once those words were out of Dr. Horne's mouth, Faye's mind began to wander. A frown crept onto her face as she lay thinking about what the doctor had just revealed to her. The words kept echoing over and over in her mind. . . . "You may never walk again. You may never walk again."

Her first reaction was one of disbelief. "How can this man tell me that I am never going to walk again," she thought. "Walking isn't something that you have to think about doing. It's something that you just do! How can I not get up in the morning, swing my feet to the floor and just walk?" she wondered incredulously.

Up until this point Faye had spent her entire life being active. She had participated in every recreational sport that was available to her throughout high school and college and continued to play softball as an adult. On top of that she was a high school basketball coach.

"How am I going to show my players how to execute a new play, or how am I going to challenge them to do something that I can't do myself?" she wondered. "How do I accept the possibility that I have to spend the rest of my life in a wheelchair?" she thought as numerous images continued to float around inside her head.

As Dr. Horne's voice droned on, Faye's mind continued on its downward spiral. The neurologist was explaining in detail the exact nature of Faye's injuries, but she was far removed from the sound of his voice. She had descended to a place where all of her worst nightmares were real. Gone was the hospital room with numerous machines beeping and hissing in the background. Also gone was the doctor who was trying in vain to explain every injury that she had incurred. The only thing on Faye's mind was the fact that she was lying here in a hospital bed and here is this man—a complete stranger telling her what her future would be, telling her that this accident had taken away her ability to play basketball, softball and more importantly, walk. Forever. In his version of her future she was banished to a place where wheelchairs were a part of everyday life. The words "quadriplegia" and "paralysis" were normal parts of speech.

This realization hit her with great force, and for a short while Faye was overwhelmed with sadness and confusion. "How could something like this happen to me" she thought. "My life will never be the same without the use of my legs."

Although she didn't know what to feel, crying was not something that she thought about doing. Instead she prayed. *"Lord, please guide me. Help me to be strong. I know what the doctor said, but I'm asking you for a second opinion. I need you to help me get through this. He is just a doctor. He is a man, and he is only saying what he is supposed to say. My faith tells me that I can do all things through you. Help me to be strong for Mother. She is not going to handle this well."*

"Miss Baker, do you have any questions?" Dr. Horne asked, interrupting Faye's chain of thought.

"No, I just want to see my family," she replied.

As Dr. Horne made his way to the door, Faye continued to think about what she had just been told. She was trying hard to wrap her mind around the fact that something of this magnitude had happened to her. How could it happen to her, she thought, to Faye Baker, athlete and coach? Letting out a deep breath that she seemed to have been holding in forever, she once again closed her eyes in prayer.

"Lord, only you know what's best for me. Only you can determine what my future is going to be. If this is your will, then I have to obey. But until I know for sure what you want for me, then I am going to have to just wait and see. Please keep me strong. And please help me to be able to tell my family about my injuries. Keep them strong. This I ask in your son's name. Amen."

9 / Faith

WHEN HENRY BAKER ARRIVED at the hospital parking lot, his eyes came to rest on the figure standing outside the emergency room entrance. "Oh God," he thought, don't let it be." Sandy Williams was standing solemnly on the sidewalk with his hands behind his back. He had been patiently awaiting the arrival of the Bakers. It was his job to lead them to Faye.

Without asking any questions, they silently made their way to the family waiting room. Inside the room were several friends from church and numerous family members. Among them were Faye's cousins, Stephanie, Helen, Yvonne and Harold Woods. They were standing silently, speaking in hushed whispers, trying desperately to hold back tears. As Faye's parents came into the room, everyone marveled at how they could continue to be calm in the wake of the doctor's revelations. As Mrs. Ethel hugged each family member, she didn't notice the tears in their eyes or the pitying looks that each one gave her. She would later say, "God must have temporarily blinded me, because I never saw the tears."

The family waited a short period before a doctor was available, then they proceeded to the family conference room.

"I'm sorry to report that there has been no change in

the patient's condition,"the doctor reported. "Miss Baker has suffered a fracture of the C 6/7 vertebrae and crushed her spine. I have already informed her about her paralysis."

"Paralysis! What paralysis" asked Mr. Baker? All eyes turned to HC. Turning to her father with tears in her eyes, 15-year-old Chandra Baker shouted "Daddy, you lied!" as she burst into tears, along with her grandmother, Ethel. Hugging his daughter, HC tried to comfort her as best as he could. He tried to explain that he had lied because he knew they would not be able to handle the news at that time. He was worried about how his parents would handle this news, and he just wanted to ease their sorrow—if only for a little while.

One thing HC would later realize was that he had very little to worry about when it came down to his father. In fact, moments after the doctor gave them the devastating news the patriarch of the Baker clan let it be known to everyone within earshot that his was a family anchored in the Lord when he proclaimed "Dr. Horne, no offense to you, but we know another doctor." After which, he guided his wife out of the room.

While walking down the corridor, one thing kept echoing through Ethel's mind. The words "I have already informed Miss Baker about her paralysis" was nagging at her. "How could he tell Faye something like that without any support?" Ethel wondered angrily. "I know I am going to find my child in tears. He should never have told her something like that without family around." Her motherly instincts kicked in, and the only thing she could think about was comforting her daughter. She had forgotten all about her grief at what the doctor had said as she rushed down the hall in search of Faye.

Facing her family for the first time, Faye told them "Well, it doesn't sound good." As she prepared to tell them what the doctor's prognosis was her brother HC stopped her immediately.

"But it is good. God has the final say!" he said with sheer determination shining in his brown eyes.

"As long as you have life, you can get better", her mother added.

Ethel had come in the room prepared to find Faye in tears, but instead she was greeted by something totally different. Faye seemed to have taken the news in stride. There were no tears. Instead, she repeatedly told everyone how grateful she was to be alive.

Surrounded by family, Faye felt safe and protected. Although the doctors said one thing, she had heard from the "experts" and they said it was going to be all right. Therefore, she knew it would. "My mother said that I could walk again. I have always believed the things that she told me and that day wasn't any different," she would later explain. "From the moment those words were spoken, they became gospel for me. From that point on, I was surrounded with a quiet peacefulness. I knew no matter what *they* said, I was going to walk again. My attitude became one of it's not about if I would walk again, but when I would walk again."

10 / Spinal Fusion Surgery

They Said

They said it could never happen; that it will never be.
But they evidently don't know my God and
the plans he has for me.
They say "I can't," but my father says, "Yes you can."
All I need is my faith and a firm grip on my master's hand.
He will walk beside me or carry me if need be.
But I will rise again; just you wait and see.

*L*ATER ON THAT EVENING the medical personnel assigned to Faye's case met with the family to further discuss her injuries and the few treatment options that were available. Again, the fractures of the 6th and 7th vertebrae were discussed. In basic terms, the bones were crushed, and without those bones in place the head has less support than that of a newborn baby.

Spinal fusion surgery was scheduled for the following day. It was the consensus of the doctors that this surgery was going to make life a lot easier, but it wasn't going to do anything to change the paralysis. It was going to prevent Faye from wearing a halo, a metal apparatus that supports the head and takes pressure off the spine. It's called this because it resembles an angel's halo.

The surgery was necessary to make sure no further damage is done to the spine. The paralysis—according to the doctors—,was here to stay. The best thing they could do for Faye, the surgeon explained, would be to train her to be self-reliant. But Faye had another agenda. She had made up her mind that she was going to walk again.

⚜

October 23rd dawned sunny and bright, but for the Baker family it was a day filled with anxiety. Calls had been placed to Faye's sister Barbara in Chicago and to her brothers' homes in Atlanta. Lily had phoned Ronald, and he in turn phoned everyone else. HC manned the phones at the hospital because numerous calls were coming in from family members, co-workers and friends. It seemed that a whole town was on alert. Everyone was concerned about the welfare of this beloved basketball coach.

In Allenhurst, Mr. and Mrs. Baker rose extra early. It was very important for them to make it to Memorial on time for Faye's 9:00 a.m. surgery. As they made their way onto I 95, they could see traffic moving at a slow pace, which dismayed them greatly. Glancing at his watch, Henry Baker showed signs of irritation. He tried to remain calm as he prayed for this traffic jam to move on.

"We aren't going to make it, Henry," Ethel said as she tried to glance around the car in front of her. "What is holding this traffic up?"

Looking at his watch again, Henry decided to pull onto the shoulder of the road. "We might as well pull over and say a prayer right here since we won't make it in time," he said to his wife. Henry took both of Ethel's hands, and they bowed their heads and said a prayer for their daughter. Once the prayer was completed, a quiet calmness took over the car. It seemed as if the Holy Spirit settled in the front seat between the Bakers and was quietly soothing their troubled minds. Henry could tell that God was moving, and he smiled as he gave his wife's hand one final squeeze before looking into his rearview mirror.

They pulled back onto the highway and were soon flowing with the traffic. Reaching the hospital, the pair hurriedly made their way to the second floor. When they rounded the corner, they were pleasantly surprised to see that Faye had not yet been taken to surgery. She was lying in her bed in the hallway with Dr. Horne standing by her side.

"They're here," he said softly in Faye's direction. Struggling to open her eyes, she managed a faint smile. Having been administered a sedative, she was slightly drowsy, but she had been aware of the fact that her parents had not yet arrived.

"Hey Mother and Daddy," she whispered, as Mrs. Ethel bent over and gave her daughter a kiss on the cheek.

"I love you and God is with you," she whispered. Holding Faye's hand, Ethel fought back tears that were threatening to spill over. As the first tear made its way down her cheek, she walked away quickly before Faye could see her crying.

11 / Prayer Changes Things

SIGNING THE LAST OF THE paperwork authorizing the surgery, Mr. Baker asked Dr. Horne if it was possible for them to say a prayer together. Nodding his head in agreement, Dr. Horne took one of Faye's limp hands and one of Mr. Baker and they closed their eyes as Henry said a prayer for his daughter, as well as the doctors with whom he trusted with her life. *"Lord, we ask that you guide the hands of these doctors and Lord we know that you and only you have the power to heal,"* Henry's voice boomed. *"We ask that you be merciful as Faye goes through this process. Cover her with the blood of Jesus. Make her strong, Lord. Heal her in your son's name."*

Looking up, Henry stared intently into Dr. Horne's eyes before stating, "Now Dr. Horne, you're ready." Breaking eye contact with the perplexed looking doctor, he bent down to give his daughter a final kiss."Now, Faye, you're ready."

"OK, Daddy," she murmured, before letting sleep consume her. Later Henry would say that at that very moment, he was certain that the surgery would be successful. There was no doubt that the Lord would guide Dr. Horne's hands throughout this surgery. Henry believed in the power of prayer, and with hundreds of people praying for one common cause, he knew that they couldn't go wrong.

Prayer vigils were being held as far away as Chicago, for

Barbara Baker-Derrick was determined not to leave anything to chance. She had been attending church services on the evening of October 22. The services had not failed to leave her feeling wonderful and blessed, as they always did. She was surprised on returning home to find a message from her younger brother Ronald.

"Now, Ron knows my schedule forwards and backwards. He knows I'm in church at this time. Something must be wrong!" she thought. While listening to the message, she said a silent prayer for her family. The message simply stated that there had been an accident, that her mother was fine but Faye had been hurt.

Once she found out the extent of her sister's injuries and also about the pending surgery, she found the best prayer warriors she could locate in and surrounding the Hazelcrest section of Chicago and went on a prayer vigil. And that is what she was doing as Faye underwent four hours of Spinal Fusion surgery.

During the surgery all of the crushed bone fragments were removed and donated bones replaced the missing bones. Prior to surgery, the option of grafting bone from Faye's hipbone had been discussed, but they decided to spare her this procedure and instead use what they had. After setting the bones in place, they were supported by a titanium plate that spanned across the 5th through the 8th vertebrae. The surgery was successful.

Once she regained consciousness, Faye was in such a weakened state that she couldn't do much besides sleep. But this fact didn't stop the visitors from coming. Everyone came to see for themselves that Coach Baker was doing well.

Left: Faye as a
toddler, along
with her father.
Below: Adolescent
Faye with her
nephew Danny
and her father.

Left: Faye at age 8.
Below: Faye at her
master's degree
graduation
ceremony in 2000.

Above, left to right: Ethel, Faye and Henry Baker at Faye's high school graduation in June 1981. Left: Faye with her roommate Michelle and her goddaughter Suede.

Above, left to right: HC, Chandra, Belle and Genese Baker. Right: Faye in front of the trophy case in her parent's home.

Roomate
Michelle
and god-
daughter
Suede.

Physical therapist Robin Moss stands behind the "Diva Sisters,"
Jackie, Faye and Edna.

Left to right: Ronald Baker, his wife Mildred, and their two sons, Terrel and Jabari

Faye Baker and the author, Tamara Pray Frazier

The family gathered to celebrate the 50th wedding anniversary of Ethel and Henry Baker. Shown above are, left to right, Faye Baker, Barbara Baker, Henry Baker, Ethel Baker, H.C. Baker, Ronald Baker and Derrell Baker.

The Baker family gathered to celebrate H.C.'s master's degree ceremony. Shown here are, left to right, Ethel Baker, Derrel Baker, Genese Baker, H.C. Baker, Chandra Baker, Ronald Baker, Henry Baker, and Barbara Baker Derrick. Faye Baker is seated.

Plotting their strategy: Faye Baker (facing the camera), 9th grade coach Vivian Gilliard (in white). Standing players, left to right, Melia Sherman, Paris Campbell, Cameren Farr.

Seated beside Coach Baker, facing the camera, is Dominique Dickerson. Sabra Blackwell (20), Tamekia Powell (4) and Charee McGirt (15) are sitting with their backs to the camera.

Assistant Coach Warnella Wilder (left) and Faye Baker coaching the Tigers in the state semi-finals, played at Georgia Tech.

12 / Tears From the Tigers

WALKING THE HALLWAYS OF Bradwell Institute on October 23, one would have been hard pressed to locate one person who was not feeling the effects of the accident that had taken place on I-95. Morale was low among the students, as well as the faculty. Tears were abundant, and it was not uncommon to see students or teachers huddled together deep in conversation. Hugs were plentiful, and any restriction on prayer in schools went out the door. Everyone was worried about Coach Baker; the fun-loving teacher and coach who always had a ready smile and never seemed to be in a bad mood.

Lillie Kelly, the girls' track and volleyball coach and a close, personal friend of Faye's, had heard from several coworkers that Faye had been in an accident, but she did not understand the severity of it. "I was not willing to believe that this could have happened. Faye was like a younger sister to me, and I could not even fathom anything bad ever happening to her," she recalls. It wasn't until Latoya Horton, one of the basketball players, delivered her version of the accident that reality began to set in for Coach Kelly, who immediately assembled the girls' basketball team for a meeting.

"Ms. Kelly, are you going to take over and coach us until

Coach Baker gets back?" Brittney Campbell asked. Brittney was one of the five starters on the team, and she had been playing under Faye's leadership for several years. She was having a particularly hard time adjusting to the fact that her coach was hurt, and having to deal with a new coach was not something she looked forward to.

"No sweetheart, I won't be able to do that. I am not a basketball coach, but I will be here if you all need me for anything," she replied.

"Right now we don't know who is going to coach you, but we will let you know as soon as we find out." This voice came from Jim Walsh, the athletic director at Bradwell.

As the girls shifted uncomfortably on the gym's bleachers, Coach Kelly and Coach Walsh tried to relay all the information that they had been given. "We know this is a hard time and we know that you love Coach Baker. We all love her, but we have got to try to keep moving forward. You know that's what Coach Baker would want. I will make sure to let you all know whenever I hear anything," she told them, knowing how important that was to them.

As Coach Walsh continued on where Mrs. Kelly left off, he could see the sadness in each set of eyes that stared back at him. He knew that no matter whom they lined up to replace Faye, the transition would not be an easy one. Therefore, he appealed to the loyalty they had for their coach when he told them, "The best thing that you can do for Coach Baker is to make her proud. Move ahead with what you all started."

"That's right," Mrs. Kelly chimed in "show everybody what you're made of."

Coach David Jones, the boys' head basketball coach remembers meeting with Coach Walsh. "We had decided that we would do whatever it took to make sure that the team would be one less thing for Faye to worry about. See, we knew the kind of dedication that Faye has, and we knew that despite her injury she would be more worried about her girls than about herself," he remembers. "Rhett Helgren, the boys' assistant coach, and everyone in the athletic department agreed to pitch in and do whatever we could. Our thoughts leaned towards Janet (Reddick) as a replacement, but we knew she was not coaching because she did not want to be coaching, so we were hesitant to bring it up to her."

The fact, however, was that coaching this team was precisely what Janet Reddick had in mind.

13 / Parallel Lives

Parallel lives going in the same direction
along the very same street.
Traveling the same course, yet some distance apart;
Never the two shall meet.
Imagine two trains, traveling along the same trail,
On the same course, but on a different rail...
Lightning strikes! One train's course change,
Touching the lives of many, including the parallel train.

*J*ANET REDDICK HAD BEEN the head basketball coach at Bradwell Institute for ten years before she retired from coaching in 1993. She had also played basketball and softball at Georgia Southern, just as Faye had done. She had coached some remarkable athletes, including Delisha Milton-Jones (Los Angeles, Sparks) and our very own Coach Wilder, the assistant to Coach Baker.

Janet decided to give up the high pressure of her coaching position after ten seasons to "give myself some time to enjoy life." For her, coaching was a twenty-four hours a day, seven days a week proposition.

"When I wasn't conducting practice, or going to games, I was educating myself. I was constantly reading manuals, learning new plays and anticipating what my next move was going to be. I was continuously trying to improve things to help make my team more competitive," she remembers.

Now, for the ensuing seven years, Janet had been content sitting back and enjoying the game from a different perspective, that of spectator and fan. That is, until October 23, 2000.

As she walked the familiar route to the Bradwell Institute Tiger Den (the school's gym), Janet could feel something different in the air. Not quite knowing what was bothering her, she made her way to her office in the back of the gym. Before reaching her destination, the petite blonde gym teacher was stopped by a co-worker.

"Hey Janet," she called out.

Janet stopped and turned around. Smiling at her, Janet was about to say good morning when her co-worker stopped her in her tracks. Normally, Janet has a sharp memory, but even to this day she has no recollection of who it was who delivered the bad news.

"Have you heard about Faye's accident?" the faceless person asked. Immediately,

Janet's whole mood changed. The look in her blue eyes became intense. "What accident?"

"Well, Faye was in an accident. I don't know whether it's true, but they said she's paralyzed," she said before leaving Janet to her own thoughts.

Practically running, Janet went to her office to put down her things before going in search of information. "Everyone was discussing the accident, but no one had any idea as to the extent of her injuries. I don't think anyone knew how serious the accident had been, because no one had actually been there (the hospital) to see her," she later recounted.

All the new information that Janet was able to gather ultimately pointed back to what she had originally been told. Faye was in fact, paralyzed.

As Janet sat down to try to organize her day, her mind kept going back to her co-worker's plight. "What can I do to help," she wondered. "I know she's going to be out of work for a while, so maybe there's something that I can do to ease some of her worries." Reaching a conclusion, she released a long sigh. At least for the time being, she had the solution to one problem.

❦

The day that Janet Reddick and Warnella Wilder went to Memorial Medical Center to see Faye will forever be imprinted in the minds of both of them. Although Janet had already heard numerous recounts of Faye's prognosis, she was not prepared for what she saw when she walked into her room.

"I got the shock of my life! Faye was laying flat on her back and the only thing she could move was her lips and her eyes," Janet remembers. She remembered her lips because when they walked in, Faye smiled. Immediately Janet's mind went back to the previous Friday when she and Faye had stood outside the gym discussing her new basketball players. "She was standing. She was standing," Janet was thinking. "Not a week ago, Faye was walking around, joking and now she's here with a broken neck and paralyzed."

Janet glanced over at Warnella, who was standing beside Faye's bed. Since she was a semi-pro bodybuilder, Warnella

Wilder's rock hard build might cause the casual observer to appraise this woman was tough as nails and one who could handle anything, but beneath this exterior, she was slowly breaking down. Seeing her coaching mentor in this position had shaken her to the core.

"Hey, Faye, you hanging in there," Warnella asked, her voice trembling.

"Yeah, I'm hanging in there," Faye answered with a smile. As she moved her brown eyes to the location where Janet stood she murmured, "Hey, Coach Reddick," snapping Janet out of her trance. She had been thinking, "What if that was me lying in that bed?"

As she forced herself to look back into Faye's eyes, Janet remembered thinking to herself, "My God she is strong. Look at what she's going through, and she's still smiling." As always Faye was her same humble self, and Janet couldn't help but to marvel at her strength. "Instead of feeling sorry for herself, she was trying very hard to make us feel comfortable, so I tried to put on the happiest face that I could."

"Warnella, how are the girls doing?" Faye asked in a barely audible voice. With each breath, the ventilator that she was hooked to would hiss, making everyone aware of the hardship Faye was enduring.

"They're going to be fine," Warnella answered. "Of course they're worried about you, but they'll make it through."

"Well, you tell them for me," Faye whispered "that- I- am- fine. Tell them that I made it through this and I made it through for a reason."

In her eyes, determination shone like a lighthouse in the dark of the night. Leaning in closer, both Warnella and

Janet looked at Faye expectantly. As the vent continuously hissed in the background, its insistent noise seemed to fade with Faye's next statement. "I made it through because I have a job to do. I'm going to win souls for Christ," she said. "That's my purpose," she finished to Warnella and Janet's amazement.

Initially, the visit was awkward because neither Janet nor Warnella knew what to say to their friend. They both wanted to say something, but what could you say to someone who had gone through this kind of trauma? At the time, nothing seemed to be the right thing. Instead of trying to continue to make conversation, both women let Faye lead, and like magic, they soon reached a topic that was comfortable for them all: basketball.

"Faye, I was thinking. I could coach the team for a while, at least until you're ready to come back," Janet said. She had been thinking about this since the day that she found out about the accident. Even though she was content not coaching, she wasn't the least bit hesitant in her decision. It wasn't something that required a second thought. She was going to do this.

As Faye looked up at Janet, relief shone in her eyes. It felt like a weight had been lifted off of her chest. Since the day of the accident, she had been thinking of asking Janet to do this, but she, like everyone else, was hesitant. Janet had always been well respected as a coach and there was little doubt that she would lead the team in the right direction. However, what did worry Faye was how her team would receive Janet.

"Thank you, Janet. I've been worried about who was

going to coach the girls. Warnella, you know if you were certified, that would have been the easiest thing for everyone, but I guess it's all for a purpose," she said eyeing her assistant coach. Lowering her head, Warnella smiled a reluctant smile to let Faye know that she had gotten her message (*Go back to school!*) loud and clear.

Laughing out loud Janet stated "Well, you don't need to worry about it anymore. Save your strength for your recovery. Let me and Warnella do the worrying about the team," she added in her southern drawl. "I'll try not to," Faye answered reluctantly. "I know you all will do well. I have faith in you," she said hoping to give Warnella an extra dosage of reassurance.

Although she knew that Janet could handle anything that was thrown her way, the welfare of the coaching staff and players of the B.I. Lady Tigers was a constant source of worry for Faye. This, though she channeled into a source of strength and determination to move forward with her therapy. With this decided, Faye was able to concentrate on her therapy and Janet Reddick, once again (unofficially) became the head coach of the Lady Tigers.

Listening quietly to the exchange between Janet and Faye, Warnella was again struck at how strong Faye was. "I have every reason to look up to her," she thought. "She is everything that a mentor should be." As she took her turn to say good-bye she heard Faye's raspy voice. Moving to her side, she listened earnestly. "Warnella, you know I love you. You're like a little sister to me. I have confidence in you. You'll do fine," Faye whispered. "I love you, too" Warnella replied in a choked voice, more determined than she had ever been to receive her certification.

After a short visit, the two ladies left, but before the door could shut completely, they looked at each other and simultaneously burst into tears. For Janet this was a moment she will never forget. It was very emotional and it forced her to stop and look at her own life. "Faye and I have always had similarities. We attended the same college, participated in the same sports, and somehow ended up at Bradwell Institute coaching the same team-just some years apart. It could've just as easy been me. I could be the one lying in that hospital bed. At that moment, I started facing my own immortality. I started asking myself how I would handle something like this. Would I be able to move forward with my life? Would I give up? Could I remain optimistic in the face of something this tragic?" Not being able to answer these questions, Janet shook her head as she walked to her car.

Making her way home, Janet pondered the question of how it takes something this serious to make a person aware of the little things that we often take for granted. As often as the phrase "tomorrow is not promised to anyone" is used, she realized, people never think that it applies to them. Today, Janet learned that tragedy doesn't discriminate. Tragedy doesn't look for certain people, people from any particular socioeconomic background or a certain race or age group. Tragedy can strike anyone at any time and when it does, we may live to see tomorrow, but there's no guarantee that we'll see it through the same eyes as we did yesterday.

Look at Faye; she is a well-liked person. She spends extra time doing activities with children. She's a coach. She attends church on a regular basis, always kind and polite and tragedy still sought her out. It was very eye opening. "The strange thing is, she's taking this so well," Janet thought. "It's almost as if she understands why this happened and she's been reassured that it's going to be OK. Maybe... just maybe she knows something that we don't know."

No matter how hard Janet tried to understand why this would happen, the only thing certain at this point was that God was in control of this situation and He would move when he was ready—in his own time. But in the meantime, she was once again a coach.

"Lord, help me make it through this season," she prayed, with a light chuckle in her voice.

14 / The Phone Call

ACOUPLE OF DAYS LATER, HC was settling in for the day at his sister's bedside, as was customary. The family had fallen into a routine where Mr. and Mrs. Baker came in the morning. In the afternoon they were sent home and replaced by Michelle, Belle, or HC. This system was working well for everyone. This way no one suffered from burnout, yet still there was always someone with Faye.

On this particular day in the ICU, HC sat quietly at his sister's bedside. As the curtain opened, he turned to watch a nurse come in. In her hands she was carrying a tray full of juice. "Oh good" HC thought. "I am a little bit thirsty. I know Faye can't drink all of that juice."

"I just thought she might want something to drink when she wakes up," the nurse said as she put the juice down and exited the ward.

A short while later Faye woke up. "Hey, Bubba" she said.

"How are you feeling," he asked. "Are you thirsty? The nurse left you some juice."

"Yeah, I am kind of thirsty," Faye replied.

HC took a straw and held the first can of juice for his sister to drink. Once she was finished, she asked for another one. One by one the juice disappeared until all of the cans were lined up, empty, on the tray. Disbelief shone in HC's eyes as he shook his head. After a few seconds he burst into laughter because one thing was for sure, the girl definitely had not lost her appetite.

After Faye had dozed off, the phone rang. Jumping quickly to answer it before it aroused Faye from her sleep, HC snatched it from the hook. It was Al Williams, a family friend who was also a local politician. He had called to check on Faye's condition but also he wanted to know if the family had started looking for a rehabilitation center. Soon Faye would reach a point where she had received all of the beneficial treatment that Memorial could offer. He was calling to recommend a center that he had heard about, the Shepherd Center for Rehabilitation, located in downtown Atlanta. He urged the family to consider this place when they started looking. The only negative thing about the center is there was always a long waiting list.

"This was definitely the place for Faye" HC would later remark. Immediately after conferring with his family, he saw to it that Faye was put on the waiting list for the Shepherd Center.

❧

Upon arrival at the hospital, spinal cord injury patients (SCI patients, as they are called) are immediately assessed. The American Spinal Injury Association (ASIA) uses certain guidelines to classify victims of paralysis, ranging from ASIA-A through ASIA-E. The ASIA-A classification includes patients who have no sensory or motor function. These are the ones who are diagnosed as having suffered "complete" injuries, injuries that preclude their ever walking again. ASIA-E patients are those who have sensation below the point of injury and thus have a chance to make some form of recovery. Faye was classified as ASIA-A.

In the ensuing days Faye began doing physical therapy on her lower body. She was extremely weak and had to rely on someone to do things that we often take for granted. She could not bathe, brush her teeth or use the restroom. It was very frustrating. Faye was having extreme difficulty trying to will her body to do the simplest tasks. It took enormous effort just to sit up and put her feet on the floor—even with assistance. The first time she sat up, she became dizzy and disoriented. She later found out that this happened because her legs could not move and her muscles were inactive. It takes muscle movement to pump blood back to the heart and without that blood flow to the heart, dizziness occurs.

Faye knew that she had a long road ahead of her. Negativity was always looming around every corner, but she knew that she had a lot of people counting on her. Giving up was just not an option. As always, she turned to the Lord to help her through. He in turn blessed her with a supportive family and a support system of friends who were not going to let her falter.

15 / Aftermath of Surgery

NUMEROUS FRIENDS, CO-WORKERS and family were visiting Faye on a daily basis. Her brothers had come from Atlanta and her sister had flown in from Chicago. Being surrounded by so many well-wishers really lifted Faye's spirits. On many occasions she recalls people telling her that her attitude was helping them handle the situation. She would only smile and think to herself, "If only they knew. I'm drawing my strength from them."

During the days that followed her surgery, Faye's mind turned to basketball. Each day she would ask Michelle questions concerning her team. She was worried about how they were handling her accident.

As the head coach of the varsity girls basketball team at Bradwell Institute, Faye spent a tremendous amount of time with her team. Most of them had come to the program as freshmen and had been playing together for years. Faye remembered how, the summer before the accident, she, as a coach, and several team members had begun to mature in the game. Several of them had participated in the summer league (AAU) and had attended basketball camp. "I saw some really good things, and I was excited about the upcoming season." she later recounted. The team was looking forward to a good year, and at the time of the accident, had been going through try-outs. Faye felt that both she and the team had been cheated, and she didn't want to be separated from them. She wasn't just their coach. She was their mentor and friend. They counted on her for so much more than coaching.

Once Faye was moved from the intensive care unit, the principal at her school (Daryl Dean) and the athletic director, Jim Walsh, came for a visit. Standing over Faye's bed, Coach Walsh looked down at the basketball coach that he had so much respect for. "How're you doing, Faye," he asked in his familiar southern drawl.

"Oh, I'm doing as well as can be expected," Faye replied. She was glad to see her co-workers, especially Coach Walsh. She knew he would be able to tell her what was happening with her team. As soon as she saw an opening, she questioned him.

"Coach Walsh, what's going to happen to my team? What are we going to do?" Faye asked.

"Now Faye, don't worry about that. We just want you to concentrate on getting better. David (Jones) and I are working on that right now," he answered.

"Yeah, Coach, you don't need to worry about anything back at Bradwell," Dr. Dean added. "Your job will be there when you get better and the team will, too," he continued with a smile.

"I sent Michelle over to Coach Jones' house to let him know what was going on," Faye replied.

"Well, like I said, we have a few things in the works. Do not worry, Faye," Jim said emphatically.

After the visit, Faye continued to receive well-wishers from her job and church. The continual support was just the fuel Faye needed to add to the sparks of determination that she had burning in her spirit.

For approximately a week longer, Faye stayed at the hospital in Savannah. During this week, the family was witness to several blessings. First of all, Faye began to have burning sensations in her right leg. Although these sensations caused her pain, it was a welcomed pain. The fact was, she was feeling *something*. Though the doctors discounted it because she was still unable to feel a pinprick, this did not deter the family. They knew that their prayers had not been in vain. It was in the air. Blessings had been raining down on Faye and her family since the day of the accident. The family never stopped giving God all the glory and for this He never stopped delivering.

The next blessing came before anyone thought it would, but nevertheless, as always, it was right on time. Having decided that the Shepherd Center was where the family wanted Faye, she was put on the waiting list, which normally is extremely long. However, approximately a week after her name was added to the list, the family was notified that there would be a representative from the center in Savannah on Friday to interview Faye for *immediate* entrance to the facility!

How had this happened? Ask Ethel Baker and she'll tell you, "God can make a way out of no way."

16 / Home Away From Home

 $\mathcal{T}$ HE SHEPHERD CENTER IS an Atlanta-based catastrophic care center. It is located in the Buckhead area of Atlanta. It treats people with spinal cord injuries, brain injuries, and all types of neuromuscular illnesses. The center is the country's largest rehabilitation center and it boasts one of the highest success rates in returning its patients to their homes after being discharged. An important factor in the treatment that is received at the Shepherd Center is the fact that a family that suffered the paralysis of one of its loved ones founded it. Because they have lived through a life-altering injury, the programs are tailor-made for the comfort and ease of both the patient and their family.

The only thing that Faye was cautioned about during her interview was the fact that the Shepherd Center was no "luxury hotel," as her room at Memorial Hospital was. This was a statement that brought rounds of laughter from the Baker family and also tears of joy because they didn't care about the accommodations. The only thing they cared about was seeing Faye walk again. The fact that the center is based in Atlanta was yet another piece of good fortune, because Faye had two brothers and their families who lived there. She would always have family close by.

Before leaving the hospital, the representative from the

center asked Faye, "So, who's coming with you to Atlanta?"

Without hesitation Faye answered "Mother and Daddy."

For the Bakers, that settled it, they were going to Atlanta.

Lying in her hospital bed at Memorial, Faye's waking moments alternated between thinking about her basketball team and going to Atlanta. She would be transferring within a week, and for some reason she knew that this place was going to be good for her. For starters, she would see her brothers, Ronald and her childhood nemesis, Derrell, on a daily basis. Both of them lived within thirty miles of the Shepherd Center.

The brothers had made it to the hospital a few days after Faye's accident and had been a source of comfort for Faye, as well as her parents. No one wanted Mr. and Mrs. Baker to have to stay out all night, so every night they would take turns staying overnight at the hospital, along with the siblings, Michelle and Cynthia, childhood buddy Debbie and Faye's college roommate, Sharon.

They spent nights by her bedside quietly laughing at all of their childhood antics. Derrell, especially, had a lot of memories of times together with Faye. He is four years older than she is, and for a long time, they were the only two left in the house, a house with one television, I might add.

Derrell still laughs when he recounts how he and his baby sister, whom he affectionately calls "Cleats," fought over everything. "We got into arguments most often about the TV, but we didn't get along playing games, or anything else. When I was thirteen, we got into a big fight over coloring Easter eggs. Faye yelled 'Don't you have any friends your own age? You're too old to be coloring eggs!'"

Some of our biggest fights were over who would pick the Saturday morning cartoons. We finally came to the understanding that whoever got up first would pick the shows. It worked, too," he said. "I got to pick all the shows, that is until she realized that I was sleeping on the couch in order to be the first one in the living room," he added with a laugh.

When asked why he calls Faye "Cleats," Derrell told the story of the first year Faye started playing softball. Ethel bought Faye's first pair of cleats. She was so happy to have her softball shoes that she never took them off. She wore them everywhere. One day Derrell and his buddy Larry Riles were sitting in the kitchen. Faye walked by in her cleats and both boys glanced at her as she passed. As she passed back by, still wearing her cleats, Larry watched her pass, again. On her third trip Larry looked at Faye with a puzzled expression on his face and said "Dang, does she ever take those shoes off?"

Derrell just shook his head and explained that she wore them all day, everyday and would pitch a fit when someone tried to get her to take them off. On Faye's next trip through the kitchen, Larry said, "What's up, Cleats," and the name stuck.

Barbara also had her share of funny stories about her baby sister, who is fifteen years, her junior. She fondly remembers the time when Faye was four or five years old and Barbara was getting dressed to go to her job at the daycare center. As she continued to get ready for work she heard Faye's small voice yell out "She ain't going today!"

"Faye was standing at the door looking out and my ride was backing out of the yard," she laughed. "I had to run outside to catch my ride," she added wistfully before saying, "That girl loved being around her big sister."

Everyone enjoyed listening to and telling those old stories. Keeping everyone upbeat was no easy task, but with plenty of visitors from Faye's job and a constant stream of family and friends visiting, the job was made a lot easier.

Visitors and well-wishers came in on such a constant basis that the Bakers had to start limiting the visits. Because she was in such a weakened physical state, anyone who was not a relative or a close friend had a difficult time getting past Mr. Baker. He would lovingly explain that she needed her rest and was not allowed any more visitors for the day, but that the family would relay their concern and well wishes.

17 / Transitions

*D*URING THAT SAME WEEK, Faye spent her free time mentally preparing herself for the transition from a hospital to a rehabilitation center. She knew that she would be up against a lot of negativity because she had yet to hear anything positive from the hospital staff. They persisted with their prognosis that she would never walk again and that she would probably never speak above a whisper, despite the fact that she had yet to stop talking.

Faye listened to her doctors and always showed respect for them and their medical expertise. She knew she would need it in the meantime, but as for the rest of her life, she had a different agenda. She was determined to walk again. The word "can't" was not in her vocabulary.

On Wednesday of the following week, Faye was packed and ready to depart for the Shepherd Center. Numerous people came to wish her well. Her pastor, Reverend Lee, as well as several family members made the trip to Memorial to see her off. As was customary, a prayer was said before they embarked on the journey.

It had been decided that Barbara would ride in the ambulance with Faye. Since this was her first time getting into a vehicle since the accident, Faye was scared and extremely nervous. After she was mildly sedated and the drug took effect , everyone got into their cars and were off to Atlanta.

Because she was not allowed to ride in the back of the ambulance, Barbara rode in the front with the driver. Faye was excited about going to the Shepherd Center, but scared at the same time because she didn't know what to expect. She was eager to start her therapy, because she was ready to get back to her life. Having Barbara in the ambulance gave her a comfort that can only be experienced by people who really, truly love each other. And the relationship that the Baker sisters share is one that is built on mutual love, respect and adoration. In short, Barbara has a way with her sister that compares to none other. She is her protector and her best friend.

Mr. and Mrs. Baker had made arrangements to stay in Atlanta while Faye was in the rehab center. They had decided to stay until they could bring her home with them. Giving up one's home and moving hundreds of miles away is a huge sacrifice. However, for the Bakers, this was a part of life.

What makes it so easy to sacrifice for each other in the Baker family is, according to Faye's brother HC, is that "We know that the other one would do the same thing for us. It's something that we have always done." HC remembers a time when he had just recently purchased a truck, and Faye asked him (in front of a crowd) if she could take his truck and drive to Washington DC for the weekend. Now, everyone knows "nothing comes between a man and his truck," so everyone just laughed at the nerve of young girl to ask her brother for his New truck. Imagine their surprise when the laughter died down and he handed over the keys—just like that.

He did it because she would have done the same for him. And guess what, she did! The first car Faye purchased on her own (her prized Honda Prelude that she still owns to this day) wasn't a week old when HC borrowed it for an entire weekend to attend spring training with his brothers. "It's all about trust and love," Ronald Baker adds. I have always known that I could count on my brothers and sisters and my parents, no matter what."

While making the trip to Atlanta, Mrs. Baker lay back and closed her eyes. She was actually not sleeping, but she had spent so many sleepless nights since the accident that her body needed to rest. There were so many thoughts going through her head. Her wounds had begun to heal, but the ache in her heart was something that felt like it was there to stay. Over and over she heard the crashing sounds from the accident. She kept hearing that awful noise that the tire made when it blew out. These memories haunted her everyday.

Every single day she thought about that accident. She could see the van swerving and flipping. She heard everyone's cries and she constantly prayed for peace. Just a little peace, Lord. Hopefully, that would be accomplished on this trip. Atlanta was the place where her baby was going to walk again. She couldn't wait to reach the Shepherd Center because this place represented a new freedom for Faye. Ethel could just imagine her standing up and walking around like she used to a couple of weeks ago. It's funny, only ten days had passed since the accident, but it seemed like a lifetime ago. But now, they were going to the Shepherd Center and everything was going to be all right.

Ethel's anxiety was getting the best of her. Taking off her glasses, she wiped her eyes with a handkerchief. She was ready to reach the rehabilitation center and get Faye situated in her new home. Turning onto Peachtree Road, she thought, "What is it with all these streets named Peachtree? I could get lost in this place." Looking ahead, she could vaguely see a sign that said Piedmont Hospital, so she knew that they were nearing the Shepherd Center.

Walking into the center, Mrs. Ethel looked around. To her left she could see a young man in a wheelchair. Looking to her right she could see others wheeling down the corridors. This confused her because she thought that everyone who came here would be walking. These people were still in wheelchairs! For the last week she had harbored a secret hope that the Shepherd Center would perform a miracle, and as soon as Faye arrived, she would get up and walk. Feeling disappointed and more than a little bit silly, Ethel never relayed her thoughts to anyone. Instead, she acted like she was excited about being there when in reality she was disappointed beyond reason.

Continuing on down the corridor, Ethel could see photos on the walls of patients doing all kinds of activities. Some of them had walkers. Some were playing games and some of the photos showed people participating in sports activities—in wheelchairs. Shaking her head, Ethel said to herself, "That's not going to be Faye. My daughter is going to walk again."

For her part, Faye was feeling a little bit frightened. Seeing all of the patients in wheelchairs had overwhelmed her. And too, she knew that Barbara would be leaving soon and this bothered her. Up until this point she had been stronger than anyone would have expected. She hadn't shed one tear and her attitude was always upbeat and positive. "I was determined not to spend any time feeling sorry for myself, because I knew that it wouldn't do any good. As long as I stood on God's promises I knew that He would not let me down. I knew that I would walk again, but it was going to be when He was ready, so I was prepared to do what I had to do in the meantime and now was as good a time as any," she would later say. What she wasn't prepared for however, was the way she felt the next day when Barbara had to return to her home in Chicago.

"When Barbara walked out of my room," Faye says, "it felt like a part of me went with her. I didn't know her leaving would hurt as bad as it did." Though surrounded by other family members, the stress of the prior two weeks came crashing down around her and for the first time throughout this ordeal, she cried.

18 / Today I Cried

Today I Cried

Yesterday was the hardest day of my life.
A day filled with stress and undue strife.
Burdens too heavy for my fragile heart to bear,
Threatened to bury my soul under
a mountain of despair.
Today I cried, I cried and I cried;
Until those burdens just disappeared and died.
Today I cried and I cried some more,
Til worry walked out and faith burst
through the door.
Today I cried— cleansing tears from within my soul
Finally falling to my knees, letting
the Lord have control.
Tomorrow is a new day, one that the Lord has made
A day for which I have hoped and I have prayed.
Tomorrow I will breathe easier;
I will smile in spite of.
For my peace comes from heaven,
from my father above.

*B*ARBARA'S DEPARTURE WAS ONE of the hardest parts of the nightmare for Faye, as well as for Barbara. "I hated leaving Faye at the hospital. It was like I was leaving my own child. I did a lot of praying for her, as well as for my family and myself. I thank God for having me 'prayed up' when all of this happened, because I don't know if I would have been able to deal with this," Barbara reminisced. "God kept me and He made me strong so that I could be strong for Faye."

With daily phone calls and constant encouragement and praise, Faye continued to think positively and believe in the power of prayer. "Never give up" became her mantra. Even as time wore on, and nothing changed medically, the family never gave up. She was here, and as long as she was here, she could get better.

Making her way through Atlanta's busy Hartsfield International Airport, Barbara barely noticed all the hustle and bustle that was taking place around her. Stepping into the Atrium, Barbara looked around until she spied a Starbucks. After purchasing a cup of coffee, she moved blindly towards the security checkpoint. Normally in this airport she would take a minute and glance in one of the many shops that was in the airport. Sometimes she stopped in the Body Shop and purchased some lotion or a candle, but today she wasn't in the mood. She was anxious to get home to her husband. Since she couldn't stay in Atlanta with Faye, then she definitely needed to be home with Mickey. He would provide the quiet warmth that she needed desperately.

It had been a rough week seeing Faye in this shape. Taking her seat on the plane, Barbara tried her hardest to relax, but she was consumed with thoughts of her "little" sister who had long since outgrown her. She thought back to the fifteen-year wait that she had to go through before her mother had given birth to Faye.

Recalling how she had prayed for a sister during each of Ethel's subsequent pregnancies, she smiled when she thought of the day Faye was born. Although it took fifteen long years and three knuckle-headed brothers, her little sister was definitely worth the wait. As she silently checked her seatbelt and prepared herself for take off, she thought back to all the summers when Faye was coming up, how she spent every summer with her and Mickey and their son, Danny (and later they were joined by Michael Jr.).

Because she had two boys, she enjoyed having a girl in the house. "I loved having Faye come up every summer because I got to do things with her that I couldn't do with my sons. It was like we had our own daughter, and Mickey and I loved that. We shopped for her in the fall and in the spring. Sometimes I went without because I never wanted to disappoint her."

There was never anything that Barbara would not do for Faye and this grave injury was no exception.

While she was gazing out the window at the clouds, Barbara's mind wandered back to October 22. She thought about everything they had gone through so far. Barbara wanted to make sure that she had covered every base. While at the hospital and the rehabilitation center, Faye was prayed over, scriptures were read and Barbara often sang her favorite song "Have you prayed about it." Being a co-pastor of a church, she had been a witness to God's work.

"I believe in the power of prayer," she states emphatically. "It changes things, and I know this because I have witnessed his goodness and mercy." Satisfied that she had left no stone unturned, she lay back in her seat and closed her eyes.

19 / Way To Go, Cleats

$\mathcal{B}$ACK AT SHEPHERDS, THE family was in conference with the neurologist assigned to Faye's case, Dr. McDonald. Shaking his head, he echoed everything that Dr. Horne had said back at Memorial. He told the family that Faye would be paralyzed from the waist on down. He also said she would have limited movement in her arms and hands.

While he continued to tell everyone that Faye was never going to walk again, Faye herself lay there with a contemplative look on her face. The brothers exchanged looks as the doctor continued.

Ronald watched his sister closely for signs of distress. When he saw none, he moved on to his other family members. No one seemed to be taking heed of this doctor's prognosis. Everyone just listened and nodded his or her head.

Mrs. Baker was looking expectantly at her daughter because she was worried about how she would handle this latest bit of bad news. After all, how much bad news could one person stand?

Once Dr. McDonald finished his session with the family, he left to check on his other patients. "You know what Mother," Faye stated before the door could close. "Everything that he said just flew right through my ears."

"That's right, baby," her mother echoed "in one ear and

out the other." The family was so relieved to hear this coming from Faye because she had enough to deal with, just living with the injury. Imagine what her life would be like if she didn't have anything positive to hold on to. Ronald and Derrell shared a proud look that said "Way to go Cleats." At that time she sounded just like the little girl who loved to be the first one at bat, but when it was time to play the field, she would run in the house and hide. This was the little girl who would argue and fight with Derrell over any and everything. It didn't matter how much older or bigger he was, Cleats never gave up.

Wednesdays at Shepherd Center is reserved for in processing and evaluation. On Thursday, November 9th, Faye once again took the ASIA evaluation. Again it was found that her injury level was at the C6/7 vertebrae, but because of the swelling, its effects reached the C5 level. This meant there was no movement below the point of injury and only limited movement in her hands. Her wrist extensors were very weak, which rendered her hands virtually useless. Another test she was given was the *position sense* test. This test is given to find out if she could locate her limbs when her eyes are closed. When the test was administered, Faye could not locate the joints on the left side. She could not find her knee joint or her ankle. At Shepherds, she was classified as *Max Assistance*. This means there was nothing that she could do without assistance.

Once testing was completed, Faye was placed on the

Critical Team under the supervision of a physical therapist named Steve Hurd. Faye's first therapist was a tall, dark and handsome guy who had a body that spoke of numerous hours spent in the gym and weight room.

"Oh Lord, I know I'm about to get worked to death," Faye thought. Looking at his build, Faye could visualize the rough times ahead. "I saw how he was built, and I knew that he was very serious about working out. I just didn't know *how* serious until my therapy started."

The Critical Team is comprised of patients who are in the weakest physical condition. Although she was now classified as ASIA-B (because of the persistent burning sensations in her right leg), she still had no motor function and had not been able to move any body parts below the point of injury. And because of this, the goals of Faye's therapist were to teach her how to function from her wheelchair.

At this point, Faye was in such a state that she could not perform any bodily functions without assistance. It took all of her energy just to get up in the morning, so she had to contend with relying on Steve to move her limbs during therapy.

Steve never ceased to amaze Faye; she would marvel at how he picked her up and threw her body around during these sessions. "I used to think to myself that if my neck wasn't already broken, he would've broken it by now—throwing me around like a sack of potatoes *and* I was wearing a neck brace" she would later laugh.

20 / Let's Burn All the Socks!

During the morning sessions, patients were expected to wheel themselves from session to session. Given the circumstances, Faye was allowed the use of an electric wheelchair until she was strong enough to wheel herself.

During one particular therapy session, Steve surprised Faye with the knowledge that he was aware of her status as a basketball coach. Dig deep, Faye! Keep trying. What would your girls say," he prodded. "Huh? Isn't that what you tell them—not to give up." Hearing Steve mention her basketball team was all the motivation that Faye needed. Her girls needed her and she needed to be there with them.

She made sure to put forth extra effort in her therapy because she had been having a hard time completing some of the tasks that he put before her. One task in particular frustrated Faye beyond imagination. Faye's day began at 7:30 a.m. The nurse technician helped her shower, groom, get dressed and move herself from the bed to the wheelchair.

Countless mornings Faye experienced frustration at its worst. At this stage in her life when most people her age were teaching their children tasks like tying their shoes and buttoning up their shirts, Faye was now trying to learn these things over again. What had once been a chore she never thought twice about, now became her greatest challenge. It amazed her how something as simple as putting on a pair of socks now took her all of thirty minutes (and that was only one sock!).

⚜

While Coach Baker was hundreds of miles away, fighting to learn things that we adults take for granted, back in Hinesville her basketball team was struggling to adjust to life without her.

The shrill sound of a whistle blew. "Darica, move your butt!" Coach Reddick yelled across the gym. "I think as old as I am I can beat you down the floor."

"I am running," Darica mumbled as she continued to make her way down the court.

Janet had been coaching the team for a few weeks, and she was having her share of frustration. For one, she hadn't coached in seven years, and she was not used to young people voicing their opinions as strongly as these young ladies did. It seems they always had to have the last word.

"Don't talk, just run," Janet returned.

As they finished their laps one by one, the girls looked at each other. "I'll be glad when Baker comes back," Brittney remarked as she walked towards the locker room. "Why did she have to change my position anyway?" she asked.

"Brittney, I'm sure Miss Reddick has a reason for that," her sister, Paris remarked. "Let's just try to get along. You know Coach Baker would want it that way," Paris continued.

"Yeah, well I'm about an inch away from the door!"

Brittney remarked as she took off her shoes.

Although they had promised Coach Kelly that they would continue to work hard and do what they knew Coach Baker would want them to do, they were finding it was easier said than done. Some of them were having problems adjusting to a new coach, but for the most part, they just missed Faye and worried about her.

"Having a new coach was hard because we were just used to the way Coach Baker did things," Darica Howard says.

That's a sentiment echoed by Brittney Campbell. "We were used to the way she coached. It was hard for me, especially because I have a hard time getting used to new people."

Coach Reddick was trying to adjust to coaching a new generation of girls, and the girls were trying to adjust to a coach with a totally different personality than the one they were accustomed to. The most marked difference would have to be the fact that Faye has a very calm demeanor. In essence she is a "gentle giant." Even when she is angry, you would never know it from the tone of her voice. During her coaching years prior to the accident, she always had to contend with Michelle and Tamara (who both played basketball under Coach Reddick), sitting behind the bench during games sending her notes saying "Stop being so doggoned nice to them. They need to be told off!" She disposed of the notes without reading them.

Janet, on the other hand, is all of 105 pounds and is a ball of fire! Never one to bite her tongue, Janet Reddick was a loving coach, but also one to tell you in no uncertain terms what she thought you most needed to hear..

Later, everyone would realize how hard it was to step into someone else's shoes. The fact was, Janet knew virtually nothing about the girls on the team before taking over. She didn't know their strengths, weaknesses, and most importantly, she did not know their personalities. These are the things that make a coach's job easier. These are also things that are learned over time. But time was something that neither the girls nor Coach Reddick had an excess of. They were all thrown into a situation where they had to sink or swim and in the end, the dedication to the sport and loyalty to Coach Baker won out. This made for more than a few tense moments, but despite that the season was off to a good start. Some days the mood was so solemn in the gym that Warnella had to remind the girls of their coach's plight. She would lecture them on the need for tenacity in the face of adversity. Seemingly, these talks worked, for when it was game time, the Lady Tigers showed up to play.

21 / Back To School

BACK AT THE SHEPHERD Center, Faye was moving along with her therapy. She had graduated from the Critical Team and was now under the supervision of a therapist named Robin Moss. Robin was also an imposing figure.

"She worked me even harder than Steve, if that's possible," Faye says. "She was like a drill sergeant. She pushed me to the limit and beyond." Robin wasn't a therapist to stick to one drill for too long. She believed in covering a lot of ground, and as soon as her patients mastered one skill, they quickly moved on to another.

It was with Robin that Faye worked on different therapies such as bed mobility, mat mobility, hands and upper body. The one task that gave Faye the hardest time was rolling over and coming into a sitting position. "The rolling over was easy," Faye says. "It was coming to the sitting position that took me forever to learn."

What made this task so hard was the fact that Faye's upper body was weak. Faye's injury level was at the C 6/7 vertebrae, which affect the triceps. This made sitting up difficult and it also made her hands tender. For this, the therapists used a machine for electro-stimulation that helped in opening and closing her hands. Another problem Faye was trying to conquer was fighting off chills. Some days the chills got so bad that Faye would wear two pairs of gloves.

There was so much learning involved. Faye and her family had to be educated on activities of daily living (ADLs). This includes feeding, grooming, bathing, dressing, home management, communication, bladder and bowel functions, as well as sexual dysfunction. They had to learn how to administer a catheter as well as the "magic bullet," a suppository that had to be administered to regulate her bowels, which at this time had not yet began to function.

They were taught safety measures during bathing and transferring from bed to wheelchair, from wheelchair to vehicle and wheelchair breakdown, just to name a few.

Robin Moss has fond memories of the patient she nicknamed (along with the two other ladies, Jackie and Edna) "The Diva Sisters." Robin remembers taking the divas on trips through one of the many tunnels that connected the center to Piedmont Hospital. One particular tunnel is nicknamed the "Red Carpet," for its obvious red floor color.

Usually when you hear the name the Red Carpet, your mind goes to the one that is often the showplace for celebrities to show off the latest fashion couture, before famous events, but this red carpet is a completely different showplace. On this red carpet, you won't find ladies in long, sequined dresses, nor will you find handsome leading men in the finest tuxedos.

More likely, you will find spinal cord injury patients using this trek from Shepherds to Piedmont hospital as a therapeutic workout. Using a manual wheelchair was no easy task for the ladies and adding a steep ramp made the Red Carpet one of the hardest forms of therapy.

Robin would occasionally take her patients to the tunnel and have them practice going down the steep ramp while maintaining control and then going up without rolling back down. The C5 vertebrae guaranteed that Faye had the ability in her hands, but the injured C6/7 caused weakness in the wrists and biceps; thus making this task extremely difficult.

Leslie Van Hiel, the clinical research coordinator believes Faye's hard work and determination made the difference. "She never gave up. She was always willing to cooperate with her therapists. Anything they asked, she was willing to give 110%." This is a sentiment echoed by Robin. "Faye was always such a hard worker. She pushed herself to be independent," she fondly recalls. This was very important because Faye had to show remarkable progression before she would be able to do the one thing that she wanted to do almost as much as she wanted to walk again – go home.

 Before being allowed to go home for a weekend, it was a necessity for Faye and her caretakers to learn how to transfer her from the wheelchair to the car. Ronald remembers one particularly cold day that they were working on this. "It was freezing cold outside, but it was important that they learned this particular task, because everyone was anxious for Faye to go home. My parents stayed out in the cold for hours trying to get this right." Looking on as his parents stayed right there, physically participating in the activity, Ronald realized the sacrifice that his parents were making. "Just, look at them," he thought. "They are hanging in there like real troopers."

He says at that time he was inspired by them. Both of

the elder Bakers are advanced in age, with Mr. Baker check-ing in at "seventy something" and Mrs. Baker—well its im-polite to tell a lady's age, so we'll just leave that to the reader's imagination. Ronald figured if they could show that much tireless dedication, then so could he, and he started spend-ing his lunch hour at the center.

As bad as the situation was, Ronald and Derrell enjoyed having their family in Atlanta. It gave them the opportunity to see their parents and siblings on a regular basis. Ronald remembers the nights when they all would be in attendance at the rehabilitation center. They would sit around and sing songs of praise, laugh, eat and at the end of each night, they would say a family prayer.

One particular song Ron remembers Faye enjoying was "All in His Hands." The words had a great impact on Faye. "I'll put it all in his hands. No matter how big or small, he's the master of it all." They reminded her on a daily basis that God was in control.

On those evenings Ronald would be in charge of provid-ing dinner. He would often go home after a long day at his job in the accounting firm, and he and his wife Mildred would cook dinner for the entire family. Ronald says Mildred and his sons—Terrel and Jabari—were very supportive and un-derstanding about his absence. On several occasions, Ron would whip up one of the family favorites, his famous spa-ghetti. Sometimes he would also bake a cake for dessert. Ron's dinners were especially enjoyed by Faye, who never, throughout the entire ordeal, lost her appetite.

22 / Through Thick and Thin

*O*CCASIONALLY, FAYE WOULD have moments when she was alone and she would think about all of her friends back home. She often thought about her goddaughter, Suede, whom she missed terribly. Thinking back to her time at Memorial, her heart would fill up when she thought about all the people who had visited. People whom she had lost contact with, as well as students and teachers that she worked with provided a constant stream of support during this time. Faye remembered people who were virtual strangers stopping in just to let her know that she was in their prayers, and this warmed her heart.

Never far from Faye's thoughts was her circle of friends, Michelle, Cynthia, Sandra and Debbie. She had not been able to see anyone but Michelle on a regular basis, but the daily phone calls she received kept her positive. Michelle came to the center every weekend, rain or shine. Since she was Faye's roommate, she would be the one providing care in the home. This was a job she took very seriously and she never missed a weekend or a training session.

Another person who helped out tremendously was Cynthia. She was unable to make the trip to Atlanta often, but she was a champ when it came to the telephone. She called every evening to get updates on Faye's progress.

Cynthia was astonished at how optimistic Faye was when she called. She never seemed down or depressed and this puzzled Cynthia. She would periodically wonder why she would always sound so enthusiastic. Soon, she would find out.

As she rounded the corner, Cynthia was trying to fight off nervous feelings. She was seeing Faye for the first time since she had left Memorial Medical Center. The last time she had seen Faye, she was in pretty bad shape. She was weak, and she had to be assisted with everything. It was so hard for Cynthia to look at Faye in that condition and she remembers crying a lot during those first weeks. She had been praying for Faye's recovery every day since.

As she walked down the hall, her thoughts returned to the night that Michelle had phoned her with news of the accident. She had been getting ready for bed when the call had come in. As Michelle recounted the details, Cynthia could feel the life draining out of her. Her heartbeat had begun to accelerate as she paced the floor. "How can this be," she wondered. "I just spoke to her before she left for the trip." As she hung up the phone, Cynthia sank down on the bed and cried.

Now, arriving at the door to Faye's room, Cynthia shook her head to clear her mind. She wanted to be strong when she saw Faye. She clearly remembered the first day after her surgery. Faye did not look good, and it took all of Cynthia's strength to make it through the visit without breaking down. She didn't want a repeat of that visit, so she took a minute outside the door and said a short prayer.

Pushing the door open, Cynthia found the room empty. She let out the breath she had been holding in. Remembering the waiting room that she passed on her way in, Cynthia back-tracked. "I'll just wait right here for her. I guess she'll be back soon," she thought as she took a seat on the floral sofa.

Rifling through a stack of magazines, Cynthia snorted in disgust. "*Ladies Home Journal, Readers Digest, Popular Mechanics*, these are the worst magazines" she said out loud. Wrinkling up her nose in disgust, she looked at another magazine before dropping that one in the pile, also. Just when she had decided to give up finding a magazine to read, she looked up and saw Faye's friend Debbie walking up the hallway. In front of her in her manual wheelchair was Faye.

"Oh my God," Cynthia exclaimed, running to the door. "You look so good!" she said bending down to hug Faye. Finding her friend sitting up in her wheelchair was stunning. The person sitting before Cynthia was light years away from the person whom she had visited in Savannah. She looked like her old self, *sans* the wheelchair.

"Surprised you, huh?" Faye asked smiling.

"You look so strong and healthy," Cynthia whispered, her eyes watering. "Now I see why you seem so upbeat," she replied. The three of them walked down the hallway to Faye's room, where they took some time and caught up on all of the latest news. They laughed and talked about Cynthia's daughters, Kayla and Shonta and how her cosmetology classes were progressing.

Cynthia was so overwhelmed by Faye's appearance that

she couldn't concentrate on anything else. She was in awe at how different Faye had become in just a few weeks time. She was thankful for these changes, because she had been extremely worried about her friend. Cynthia didn't have any doubts that Faye was strong and that if given the chance, she could recover. She was more concerned about whether or not her medical condition could get better. Seeing Faye today left her with no doubt that she was going to get better.

After her visit, Cynthia left the rehabilitation center with a new attitude. Anyone who saw her would have probably wondered why she was walking around with a smile on her face. If they had asked she would gladly have told them that "God is good." How else would a person who had been given the odds of recovery as slim to none be able to sit in front of her today, looking brand new. She was so impressed with Faye's improvement she vowed to do whatever she could to help in her recovery. Cynthia knew that Faye was going to need a lot of support from her family and friends, and she planned to be right there—through thick and thin.

In the ensuing days, Faye worked hard on her therapy. Since advancing from the Critical Team, she had become a part of the *Treadmill Research Therapy.* According to research, the human spinal cord has intelligence of its own and can generate step-like electrical patterns when exposed to sensations like walking. Body weight-supported treadmill training takes advantage of that concept by having patients who have sustained a spinal cord injury to undergo weight-supported ambulation. During this therapy, Faye was placed in a parachute harness and positioned over a treadmill. Once the treadmill belt started to move a whole team of physical therapists helped Faye to "walk."

In the beginning, the therapists had to physically move her legs, because there had been no return of function. Later, as her therapy progressed Faye would be able to pull some of her own weight. Although she had not yet regained any movement, she was sure that soon there would be a breakthrough.

As always, there was the one thing that was the driving force behind all of Faye's hard work: her team. They had recently undergone yet another transition. Just when it seemed that things couldn't get any worse, they did.

23 / More Transitions

*I*T WAS DECEMBER 2000, and coach Wilder stood before the assembled players.

"Ladies, we have some news for you. Some of you may have noticed Coach Reddick is not here today." As she looked at the girls, Coach Wilder paused before going on. "Coach Reddick had to be rushed in for emergency surgery and she's going to be out for about six weeks," she finished.

"What's wrong with her?" one of the girls asked.

"She had to have a cyst removed," Warnella answered, anxious to finish the conversation.

Standing beside Coach Wilder was Marvin Howard. At the time, Marvin was an assistant principal at Bradwell Institute. He was also serving as the coach of the ninth grade boy's basketball team. "Mr. Howard will be taking over until Coach Reddick returns," Warnella told them.

The girls exchanged silent looks that seemed to say "Not again." Although some of them didn't like making the transition from Coach Baker to Coach Reddick, the point was they had done it. She had been with them for six weeks, and they were getting used to her.

"This is getting old," Brittney remarked. "First Coach Baker's accident, then Coach Wilder had to be out for a couple of weeks because of a kidney infection, now Coach

Reddick." The girls were almost afraid to ask who would be the next victim.

This transition was yet another glitch in what most of them thought was going to be "their year". Instead, it was a year of constant battles. For these girls it was a daily struggle just to remain positive and optimistic. Although all of them knew Mr. Howard and liked him, the only person they wanted coaching them was laying in a hospital three hundred miles away, in the greatest struggle of her life.

Nevertheless, just like their coach, they were determined to do what needed to be done. They stuck together to face each opponent that stood in their way. They grew closer together as a team. This was bad news indeed for opposing teams.

"Hey ya'll, let's do this for Coach Baker," Latoya Horton said as the Lady Tigers prepared to take to the floor. They were in Brantley County, participating in the Christmas Tournament. Though they had made plans to participate in the tournament in Macon, this year they had to forego the long road trip and stick closer to home. This was a huge disappointment for them as well as for Faye. She had actually made arrangements with her therapists to attend this tournament, and she was looking forward to showing off her team to them. This was a big letdown for them, but it actually turned out to be a blessing in disguise.

As they took to the floor the same sentiment was on each

girl's heart and mind. "We have got to win this for Coach Baker." This was the last game of the Christmas tournament and the Lady Tigers had advanced to the championship round. The previous day they had defeated a team from Clinch County, which gave them a shot at the championship.

The first quarter ended with the Lady Herons on top 22-17, but after making a few adjustments on defense, the Lady Tigers came back and had a scorching second quarter. Felicia Johns led the attack with seven points and was followed closely by LaToya Horton's six. Tamekia Powell's back-to-back three pointers helped seal the championship for the Tigers.

As each play unfolded, it was obvious that these girls had more at stake than just winning to be winning. It was as if they were fighting for their lives. When the final buzzer sounded and the Lady Tigers were on top 69-56, the joy of victory was written on the face of every young lady on the team. Not only had they won a game of basketball, they had managed to hold their team together through the worst of times. For them, this victory represented triumph over adversity in the game of life. They could win, even when the cards continually stacked against them.

In the end, they dedicated this victory to Coach Baker, and each one signed the game-winning basketball to present to their coach. Looking over at Coach Howard, Warnella was so grateful that he had allowed her to have so much input. Marvin knew that the girls had already been through so much transition, so he let Warnella take on more of a hands on role. After all, she was the one constant for their team. They needed that and she was thankful that he had allowed her that space.

Later, the girls would say that it was Faye's determination to recover that was a source of strength for them. Her silent courage showed them that they could do anything that they wanted to do. It did help, however, that these young women were all strong and well-disciplined from the start. For the ones who fell a little short, there was always two or three that picked them up and helped them along. As Coach Howard would say, "They were a super bunch of girls. Their coaches before me trained them well."

24 / Video Tapes

*D*URING MICHELLE'S WEEKEND visits, she would bring along tapes from the games as a way of reassuring Faye that her girls were doing well. It was her goal to keep things as normal as possible for her roommate. She figured the tapes were the next best thing to being there.

Faye would wait anxiously for Michelle's arrival on Friday with the tapes. All week she looked forward to seeing her girls play. As soon as Michelle walked in the door, Faye would go into her "coach mode." Mrs. Baker would often sit quietly, observing her daughter's reactions, and what she saw had her worried. Faye would get so excited while viewing the tapes, her parents worried that her blood pressure would rise. After observing a particularly exciting game, in which her team made numerous mistakes, Mrs. Baker made a decision that she was sure Faye wouldn't approve of but that she knew was necessary.

"Why did she do that?" Faye yelled from across the room. Mr. and Mrs. Baker exchanged a knowing glance and shook their heads. "That was a foul!" Faye shouted. "They're beating Pre-Rook to death under the basket!" she continued her tirade, reinforcing what Mrs. Baker thought all along. The tapes had to go.

As Michelle was leaving the center for the night, Mrs. Baker walked her out the door.

"Michelle," Mrs. Baker started, "I think you need to forget the tapes for a few weeks—at least until Faye gets a little better. It's not good for her to get so excited. It's bad for her blood pressure." she stated.

Although Michelle knew what this would mean to Faye, she had to admit that Faye's parents were right. She, too, had noticed how Faye reacted. So really, there were no ifs, ands or buts. She knew the tapes had to stop, so she simply answered, "Yes ma'am," while giving Mrs. Baker a hug before leaving.

While walking back to her truck, Michelle shook her head. She was dreading having to tell Faye that she could no longer bring the tapes. As a matter of fact, before she left Faye had reminded her not to forget the tapes next week. "Oh well," she thought. "Her health is more important."

With a week to go before her next visit, Michelle decided to try to come up with an excuse later. Right now she had to concentrate on fighting this Atlanta traffic. Groaning out loud, Michelle tried to fight off the weariness that was so common with her lately. "Faye is not going to like this," she thought as she merged onto Interstate 75, the highway that would take her back to Hinesville and her daughter, Suede.

As the week neared its end, Michelle became aware that she was running out of time. She had just about run out of lame excuses. "What if I just tell her that they didn't have a chance to make a copy, or the camera broke?" she asked Tamara.

"Now, Michelle, you know Faye is not stupid," Tamara

said in a no-nonsense manner. "She's going to be angrier that you tried to insult her intelligence. I can see her now looking at you like you have two heads," Tamara laughed.

Conceding that Tamara was probably right, Michelle decided to just be honest. "You know what, I'm just going to have to tell her the truth," she said. "If she doesn't like it, I'll just let Mr. Baker handle her." As it turned out, Faye understood her parents' concerns, and she didn't give Michelle a hard time like she was expecting. Then too, not being able to see the tapes didn't deter Faye in the slightest. She still asked thousands of questions. She wanted to know the who, what, when, where and how of every game, and Michelle did her best to provide the answers. She was able to let Faye know that despite all of the ups and downs, the girls were having a stellar season.

For the coaches and players this was indeed an emotional season, but they all managed to hold it together for the sake of their coach and colleague. Not all days were great days, but all days were good days. Good, because this was a season of learning. Everyone who was involved walked away with a lot more wisdom, tolerance, patience and certainly more determination.

As far as records went, that season was one of the better seasons that Janet Reddick had coached at Bradwell, but then too, the team had talent to spare. They had Tamekia Powell, LaToya Horton, Candice Ferrell, Felicia Johns, Darica Howard, Brittney and Paris Campbell. Each of these young ladies was a scholarship recipient of some sort. Although Paris wasn't a "star" on the basketball court, (she received her scholarship in volleyball), Coach Reddick says she served a much more important role. "Paris played a key role in keeping the peace amongst the team and keeping morale up. She was supportive of me, and I really needed that. Occasionally, I butted heads with her sister, Brittney, but Paris was right there encouraging us and basically being a ray of sunshine during those dark, cloudy days."

⁂

Meanwhile, Faye was improving every day. Her strength was slowly returning, and even though there was still no movement, she was sure her patience would pay off soon. Many days in between her classes, she would hang out in her room with her roommate, Edna. Edna was from nearby Jonesboro and was also being rehabilitated for paralysis. During their time rooming together, the two women bonded because of their disabilities. Faye remembers some of those days when it was a God send having someone who was going through the same exact thing. "Unless you are in this situation, you have no idea what we go through. Edna knew what I was feeling because she was either feeling the same way or had felt that way at some point," Faye stated, matter of factly. "We worked hard to keep each other positive. We could offer advice and sympathize with each other's frustrations."

On a daily basis, Faye and Edna would come in contact with other patients who had complete injuries or who didn't have the family support that Faye and Edna did. Some of those patients felt hopeless and it showed in their actions and words. Many days Faye felt sympathy for her fellow patients, because she knew how hard it was to remain positive, even with family surrounding you. She couldn't imagine going through this alone.

Edna's family were regular visitors to the center. Everyone especially enjoyed when her grandson Brandon would come. Having Brandon around made Faye miss her seven-year-old goddaughter even more.

With each milestone that the roommates reached, they celebrated together. After leaving the center, they continued to keep in touch. "Even to this day when something good happens I have the urge to call Edna and share the news," Faye says with a faraway look in her eyes. "Sometimes in life, you form bonds that can never be broken."

In addition to bonding with a new roommate, Faye was grateful for the continued support of her roommate back in Midway. Michelle was committed to doing whatever needed to be done to help Faye recover. For people who witnessed her dedication, it was nothing short of incredible.

Michelle had had a difficult time understanding why Faye was the only one hurt, especially considering the fact that they were sitting side by side. This question was a constant presence in her mind, and kept her awake at night.

"Why did this happen to her?" she would often ask her friends. "She was always the really good one. Why didn't it happen to me?" Over time, she was able to obtain a better understanding of why Faye had been the one chosen, but at the time, she had a hard time dealing with her walking away with a scratch on her finger and her friend not being able to walk away at all.

25 / Why Not Me?

Why Not Me

So many times I've wondered, why her and why not me.
And I'm told that is the way it's supposed to be.
Yet still I wonder, "Why her? She's always so good.".
And I'm answered, "That's precisely the reason.
This needs to be understood."
Day by day it's becoming clear, why he chose her and not me.
She's strong in mind, body and faith,
as a good messenger should be.
Some of these qualities I lack, as do so many more,
So God is using her to open up the door.
Teaching us faith, endurance and patience—
things we didn't possess before.
But most importantly, to show his flock
that he CAN heal and restore.
My own faith was lacking and at times
my mind was very weak.
So now I know why I—as a vessel He did not seek.
Day by day He's opening my eyes, allowing me to see
Not only why she was chosen, but also
why He didn't choose me.

*A*S MICHELLE PUSHED FAYE'S wheelchair toward the entrance of the Shepherd Center, a smile played around the corners of her mouth. Today she and the Baker clan were taking Faye out to eat. Looking around, her eyes met Mrs. Baker's and they shared a silent look that said how appreciative Mrs. Baker was to have her here. Christmas was in a week, and if nothing came up, Faye would be making her first trip home that weekend.

As they walked through the front doors they were greeted with a crisp, cold breeze. This weather was something that they were not used to, but nothing was going to dampen the mood.

Everyone back in Hinesville was anxiously awaiting Faye's arrival. As Michelle looked at Mr. Baker, she couldn't help but to think how strong he was. Not once had his faith wavered. He held steadfast to God's promises. He didn't care what anyone else thought, because he knew his daughter was going to get better. Once again, Michelle was thankful that her mother, Lena Mae, had been supportive throughout this ordeal. She had been taking care of Suede every weekend since the accident. This allowed Michelle the opportunity to make the trip to Atlanta without fail. This she did as much for the Bakers as she did for Faye. The Baker family had taken her into their hearts and treated her like their own child. Just as Faye, HC, Barbara, Derrell and Ron worried about their parents, so did she. She made that trip every weekend, to offer them some relief as well as to help Faye. Now it seemed that all of their hard work was paying off because within a week Faye would be able to go home.

"OK, Faye, do you have everything that you need?" Faye's nurse, Velma asked in her West Indian accent. Turning towards Faye's parents, she asked, " Do you remember how we did the sliding board?" The Baker's nodded their heads in assent. "Now, are there any last questions?" she asked while looking at her list.

"Yes to the first question and no to the second," Faye replied with a bored look on her face. She was getting ready to go home for Christmas, and Velma was trying to make sure that she was well prepared. Taking a deep breath, her nostrils flaring, Faye looked at Velma. "I AM READY TO GO!" she thought as the nurse continued her constant cheerful banter.

Moving around the room, Velma continued working down her list of things to do before Faye left, seemingly oblivious to Faye's foul mood. "She is holding me up," Faye thought as she finally heard the words she had been waiting to hear all day.

"Well then, I guess you're ready to go."

Smiling for the first time, Faye decided that she wasn't mad at Velma anymore. She knew she was just trying to make sure she had covered all the bases. "But did she have to cross every T and dot every I?" she wondered.

"All right Faye, now what time are you supposed to be back on Monday?" Velma asked while bending down in front of Faye. "8:59," Faye answered, trying hard to conceal the laughter behind her frown. Faye knew she had to be back at Shepherds before 9:00 p.m. and she wasn't coming back through that door until one minute before!

As Mr. Baker pushed her through the door, Faye was both excited and nervous at the same time. She was anxious to make it back to Hinesville so she could show everyone how far she had progressed. The last time the people in the community had seen her; she was lying flat on her back wearing a neck brace. She knew her improvements were going to shock some people and she couldn't wait to see the looks on their faces.

As they neared her parents' gold Dodge Intrepid, Faye became clearly nervous. It still bothered her tremendously to get into vehicles. Though she had been required to go on field trips throughout her therapy, those trips did nothing to calm her fear. All of the trips to the mall with the staff hadn't made one bit of difference. Traveling in vehicles terrified her. The only thing that outweighed her fear of vehicles was her desire to go home. So she did what she had to do.

⚜

Arriving at the Baker household in Allenhurst, Faye was greeted by the rest of her family. Throughout the evening, she welcomed numerous visitors at her parent's home. Everyone was so excited to see how far Faye had come in the weeks since her accident.

Going to sleep that night, Faye had a huge smile on her face. Coming home felt good. Most of her basketball players and their families had been to see her, and she realized how much she missed them. The only thing that dismayed Faye throughout the day was how difficult it was to get in and out of the car. She hated having to rely on someone to do everything for her. Losing her independence was an indescribable burden. But as always, she put all of the negative thoughts out of her head and just thanked God for the little things.

As the sun peeked over the horizon and dew was still clinging to the morning grass, Faye found herself wide-awake. She had been lying in the bed trying to contain her excitement. While the rest of the Baker household was snoozing silently, Faye was thinking of all the things she was going to do once she reached her own home. Smiling like a child at Disney World, she said out loud, "I finally get to sleep in my own bed!" Silently she went over all of her planned activities. "First thing, I am going to get to see my friends, and have some fun!"

Once they reached Beaver Lane, Faye thought she was going to burst with excitement. Home! Finally! After the initial problem of getting out of the car, Faye was finally able to get inside her house. Inhaling the smell of her house, Faye was overcome with nostalgia. Just the smell of her house made her wish that she could stay home. She missed home more than anything.

"Faye, Faye did you miss your bed," Suede asked her.

"Almost as much as I missed you," Faye replied.

As Suede pushed Faye down the hallway leading to her bedroom, Faye looked at everything. She couldn't stop looking at her things. She missed everything! The pictures on the wall, the mirrors, her bed—everything! When they reached the bedroom, Michelle told Suede to step aside and let her push Faye through the small doorway. As she tried to navigate the wheelchair through the small space, she realized the doorway was too small. Knowing that there was no way to get her through the door without her wheelchair, Mr. Baker decided to take the door off the hinges. Immediately, Faye's good mood deflated. Once again she was reminded of her disability.

"They have to go through too much trouble for me," Faye thought to herself. She hated having so much fuss made over her and she longed for her old life back. She wanted to regain her independence more than anything in the world. Having to ask for help with everything bothered her, and on more than one occasion during the holiday she found herself longing for the comfort that the Shepherd Center provided. At least there she didn't feel so much like an invalid. Everything there was accessible. Nonetheless, Faye enjoyed the holiday with her family. She especially liked the spread that her mother and sister-in-law put together for their Christmas meal.

When it was time to return to the center, Faye found herself not wanting to go back, despite how hard it was to function in her "old world." Once she made it back, Faye was feeling euphoric from her trip. She had received lots of wonderful presents, but the best gift was yet to come.

26 / There's a Miracle in Store

*T*HURSDAY MORNING FAYE was lying in her bed at the Shepherd Center trying to get her toes to move. This was something that she did on a regular basis. She just knew that one day she was going to try to wiggle her toes, and they would actually move.

"Come on, God please let me feel something" Faye prayed. She knew that patience was the key but she had been here for about six weeks and had not been able to move any of her lower extremities. Discouragement was always looming, patiently waiting to jump on her back, but she was fighting it with everything she had. She had heard all the statistics; about how if she remained that way for over a month her odds of walking were about 3 percent. Faye had passed that month two weeks ago, but she refused to give up on herself and she definitely wasn't going to give up on God.

Trying again, she was puzzled when she felt a slight movement.

"Wait a minute," she said out loud. Whipping back the covers, she tried again to move her toes. Looking down at her feet, Faye could see the slightest movement in her big toe! Pressing the buzzer beside her bed, Faye tried to make her toe move again and it moved! If she could have gotten up and ran around the hospital, she would have, but she had to settle with smiling from ear to ear.

As the nurse came into the room, Faye shouted, "I think my toe moved! Or am I crazy?"

Seeing the wild, excited look on Faye's face, the nurse tried to keep her objectivity. "Do it again," she said. Concentrating hard, Faye moved her big toe for the nurse. "Well, well, well, you aren't crazy. Your toe *is* moving," the nurse replied with a big smile on her face.

Faye almost exploded with joy! "Thank you, thank you, thank you Lord!" she said over and over again. Later she would say about the perfect timing. "God may not come when you want him, but he's always right on time."

Waiting for her parents to get there at 10:00 a.m. was excruciating. Faye wanted to call everybody she knew. She wanted to shout from the rooftops, "Faye Baker is on her way!!" but she knew she had to wait. It wouldn't be fair for anyone to find out before her parents. They had been steadfast in their dedication to her and she owed them this.

As Henry and Ethel came into Faye's room, they didn't notice the way she sat looking like the cat that ate the canary.

"Mother and Daddy, guess what?" she said. Not waiting for an answer, she pulled back the cover and wiggled her big toe. "Look," she said excitedly.

"Do that again," her mother said. Faye moved her toe again. When she did this, her mother burst into tears and her father just smiled because he already knew this day was coming soon.

After telling her parents, Faye got on the phone and called

everybody that she could think of. She made enough phone calls that day to keep the phone company in business for at least another year!

One week after Faye started regaining movement and function, she moved to outpatient status. She had spent seven weeks in house and she remained a patient of the center for five more weeks before she was finally ready to come home.

While outpatient, she and her parents stayed in a room provided by the center. Even then they continuously were looked upon with God's favor. The room provided by the center had strict codes and one of the rules was that it was to be inhabited by only two persons. The room was equipped with two single beds and that was not enough space for the Baker clan. Still, having only one parent with Faye wasn't acceptable because neither Henry nor Ethel was willing to be parted from Faye.

Ethel was needed to help with Faye's hygiene and she provided that mother's love. Henry provided not only love, but also the brawn that was needed to keep Faye comfortable. Faye remembers many nights not being able to sleep because she was uncomfortable. "Daddy," she would call. "I need some help. My leg is at the wrong angle." Henry would often wake up in the middle of the night just to adjust a leg or to turn Faye over. Not once did she witness any frustration or impatience on the part of her parents. Neither did either one complain when Faye would require all of the pillows in the room in order to be comfortable.

Henry knew that having only one parent with Faye was

not an option, so he told the front desk person just as much. Well, before the evening was up, the manager had personally delivered a rollaway bed to the room for the Baker's comfort.

During therapy Faye was still working on the treadmill research, but now she didn't require as much assistance. Her right side was functioning better than the left, but she was not discouraged. Progression was her goal and that she was doing, daily.

27 / Nostalgia

*A*WEEK AFTER FAYE MOVED her toes for the first time, she was finally able to go home and see her team play. On Friday, she went to Liberty County High School to watch her niece, Chandra, play with the varsity squad. Though this was not her school, it was the school where her sister-in-law, Belle worked, and she was treated to a warm reception there.

On Saturday, Faye arrived on the Bradwell Institute campus thirty minutes prior to game time. Entering the gymnasium, Faye was overcome with wistfulness. Memories came flooding back. The smell of the gym was enough to transport Faye back to a better place and time. The girls were playing a team out of Savannah called the Groves Rebels. Faye was excited and happy to be back at Bradwell, and she was in for a big surprise before the game could get underway.

As Faye was wheeled into the gym, she was met with the familiar voice of none other than Coach Kelly. Aside from being the track and volleyball coach, Lillie Kelly also doubles as the announcer for the football and basketball games.

"Welcome, Coach Baker. Welcome back to this place...." Coach Kelly's voice filled the gym. Lillie had written and was singing a song especially for the occasion and she sang it with all the love she had in her heart for Faye.

Looking on incredulously, Faye was overwhelmed. She couldn't believe all of this was done just for her. Each one of her ball players presented her with a rose and the basketball from the Christmas Tournament. The entire night was incredible, but the best part was watching her team play. It felt really good sitting on the sidelines, and it made Faye yearn for home even more. She knew that she would be returning soon enough. Therapy had been going well and she was moving forward every day.

Janet fondly remembers the first time Faye joined her on the bench. "Faye sat beside me in her wheelchair. Not one time did she try to force her opinion on me. She let me continue to do what I had been doing throughout the season. I didn't feel uncomfortable getting onto the girls when they made errors. I have to say, I am so impressed with her," Janet expresses. "I know there were things that she probably would have done differently, but she never commented. I always felt that she must have this awesome relationship with God," she finished off with a smile.

༺✦༻

As time passed, Faye showed steady progress. After nine weeks at the Shepherd Center, Faye was now ready to go home - permanently. "I cannot even describe the way I was feeling when I went through Shepherd's doors for the last time. No, I did not walk out of Shepherds, but I left with the knowledge that walking was within my reach. I wasn't pressed," she recounts, "I knew that this happened for a reason." If she didn't know anything else, Faye knew that she had to wait on the Lord. "I knew that the plan God has for me would unfold in his own time. When He's ready, he'll move," she says matter-of-factly.

Once she returned to her home in Midway, Faye continued her therapy. She started therapy at Memorial Hospital on Monday, Wednesday and Thursday. On the other days, she went to her parents' home in the mornings. She would go over the drills that she learned at the rehabilitation center and perform them diligently.

While at Memorial, Faye did pool therapy with a therapist named Mark. Because of waters unique properties, patients experience a restorative environment that is unlike most traditional treatments. Because the body is virtually weightless in the water, Faye was actually able to stand up in the pool. The buoyancy of the water actually enables the joints to move about painlessly, so she was also able to move that unresponsive left leg.

Also, because water is resilient, it offers an excellent medium for increasing strength and endurance. The temperature of the water averages 92-94 degrees. The warmth of the water also works to decrease the pain and help relax the muscles.

In addition to the pool therapy, Faye had advanced to walking with a walker and she was working extensively on the parallel bars. She continued this regiment throughout the spring, summer and part of the fall. Sometime during the summer, HC noticed that the therapy that his sister was doing was pretty routine. After talking it over with his wife, he asked Faye and their parents what they thought about her starting to do her therapy at home instead of traveling to Savannah three days a week. HC figured with a little creativity, they could come up with similar equipment and just carry out therapy themselves. Yes, it was going to take dedication on their part and Faye was going to have to take this very seriously in order for her to be successful. She was going to have to be able to separate big brother from therapist, but HC wasn't worried about that. No one wanted to see Faye walk more than Faye herself.

Since they already had a treadmill at home, HC and Belle sat down and tried to figure out what could be used that would be equivalent to the parallel bars that Faye used to hold on to while walking. After a little creative thinking, they decided that the height of HC's truck was just about even with the bars at Memorial. Now that they had the major equipment covered, they were ready to start.

"Come on Faye," HC prodded. "You can do it," he said as they made their way down their parent's driveway. Faye was flanked on one side by Lily and on the other side, stood her father. Kneeling in front of her was HC. Since the right side was functioning at a more advanced level, Faye was virtually unable to use her left leg. To combat that HC took an ace bandage and slipped it under Faye's left foot. As she took a step with the right leg, HC would move the left. For the Baker clan, Faye's therapy was a family affair. On the days that Faye would be tired and wouldn't feel up to therapy, it was her family who encouraged her to keep at it.

28 / The Tiger Team

*A*S THE SUMMER SUN SLOWLY gave way to the cool breezes of autumn, Faye became increasingly apprehensive. She was going to return to work at Bradwell Institute and she was worried. For days, she worried about how she was going to be received. "What was the staff going to think?" As far as she could remember, she had never seen any handicap facilities at her job.

As she lay in her bed, she thought to herself, "What if I have to use the restroom? What are my students going to think when they walk in and see their teacher in a wheelchair?" she worried. She lay awake for hours wondering and worrying what her first day would be like.

Across the hallway, the same thoughts echoed through Michelle's head. She was just as worried as Faye was. "I wish I had some time off. I'd go to work with her," she thought as she rummaged through her closet. "Oh well, I guess she'll be alright," she thought as she located her work shoes. Sitting on the side of her bed, Michelle exhaled as she tied her scarf around her head. Getting down on her knees, Michelle said a lengthy prayer before taking her blanket from the foot of the bed and pulling it over her body.

After dropping Suede off to school, Michelle arrived at

Bradwell Institute shortly after Faye's arrival. Faye had recently had her driving privileges reinstated after completing a drivers rehabilitation-training program at Memorial hospital. Initially, Faye had been learning to drive using hand controls, but one Saturday she and Michelle experimented having her drive the long stretch of highway between Midway and Hinesville. When she successfully completed the trip, she reported her success to her therapists and they started letting her drive using her feet.

As Michelle pulled her dark green Mitsubishi Montero into the parking space beside Faye's Dodge Durango, she noticed something that she had not noticed before. At the point where the parking lot met the sidewalk in front of A wing, a small metal ramp had been appended. It was now handicap accessible. "Oh, that's so good," Michelle thought. "That's going to make Faye feel good," she reflected as she got out of her vehicle.

Sitting in her SUV, Faye couldn't help but smile as she patiently waited for Michelle to unload her wheelchair. Wheeling down the hallway, Faye was greeted by a chorus of "welcome backs," and "good to see you, Coach." While signing in, Dr. Dean, the principal, came around the counter to personally welcome Faye back into the fold. "It's good to see you looking so good, Coach Baker," he said. Bending down, he said in a quiet tone, "We've made sure that everything is accessible for you, so don't worry about that and if you need anything, give me a holler." Faye was put at ease by the concern and attention that she was paid all day. Just knowing that the administrative staff thought enough of her to make these modifications prior to her return made her certain that no matter what handicaps she had, she was a valued member of the Tiger team. " I left work that first day, confident in my ability to rise to the challenge," she remembers.

As basketball season rolled around, everyone was excited about the upcoming season. The team was excited to have Coach Baker back and they were looking forward to the season. For Faye, this was a particularly exciting time. She still had the bulk of her team members and though they had been derailed one season, they were all determined not to let anything stop them.

With basketball season in progress, Faye found herself having to put her therapy on the back burner. With practice in session five days a week before games started and three days a week, thereafter, there was no room left for her therapy. Aside from Sunday afternoons at her parent's house where she would do informal exercise, there was nothing regimented. Despite missing out on her sessions, Faye's balance had progressed to the point that she was able to graduate from the walker to Loft Strand crutches (forearm crutches).

By December, it was not uncommon to see Michelle pushing an empty wheelchair up the sidewalk to Faye's classroom. Shortly thereafter, Faye would slowly navigate that same sidewalk using her forearm crutches. Some of her co-workers were not aware of her progress because it wasn't Faye's habit to "toot her own horn." As a matter of fact, she enjoyed seeing the look of astonishment on the faces of her friends and co-workers.

One such co-worker had just recently moved back to Hinesville, and had joined the Project Success staff as a para-professional. She would spend her lunchtime and breaks in the classroom schedule asking tons of questions concerning Coach Baker's disability. The whole subject fascinated her and the more she learned, the more she wanted to know. All of the milestones that Faye reached amazed her. One morning she asked Faye "have you ever thought about writing a book about this because a lot of people may benefit from hearing your story? I mean, someone might be in the same boat and they may take the doctor's diagnosis as fact and just give up." Faye replied that her mother had said the same thing and just like that, the seeds for this garden were planted.

In the meantime, basketball season was in full swing and Faye had settled comfortably into her role as a physically impaired schoolteacher and coach. Every afternoon before the 3:10 bell would ring, one of her basketball players would push Coach Baker to the gym, while recounting the ups and downs of her day. Oftentimes Suede would be skipping along beside the wheelchair, speaking to everyone along the way. Since Faye had returned from the rehab center, Suede rarely left her side. It was a practice for her to ride the bus to Bradwell Institute, complete her homework before the bell rang and spend the rest of the afternoon as the manager of the Lady Tigers Basketball team. It was amazing to everyone how an eight year old knew as much about the team as any adult. She, like Faye knew their strengths as well as their weaknesses. She could remember all of the plays and could tell you when someone was out of place. Suede was smitten with basketball, or maybe it her godmother that she was so enamored with.

The date was January 30, 2002. On this night the 22-0 Lady Tigers were taking on the Camden County Wildcats. They were riding high as the number 1 ranked 5AAAAA team in the state. A few weeks prior they had been featured on a national sports show out of Atlanta. The girls and their coach knew all eyes would be on them. As they gathered in the dressing room, Faye urged the girls to keep a cool head. "It's alright to have confidence, but keep a level head. You all are the team to beat, so just concentrate on playing your game. Do not let them take your head out of the game."

As the game progressed, it was obvious that the Lady Wildcats were a team cut from the same cloth as the Tigers. They also had the momentum of a strong desire to beat an undefeated team.

At half time, the Lady Wildcats were on top 25-24. The tigers were having a hard time keeping it together, but by the end of the third quarter, the teams were tied at 39. As the forth quarter came to a close, the Lady Wildcats had made thirteen trips to the free throw line, connecting on twelve. This, compared to the five trips made by the tigers was enough to catapult Camden County ahead with a score of 57-43. The Lady Wildcats had pulled off an upset of the seemingly unstoppable Lady Tigers.

"Splat!" As everyone turned around to see what the commotion was, the Camden County Lady Wildcats were all squatted on the floor, and had slapped the floor as if to say, "Yeah, we beat the Tigers." Looking at each one of the Lady Tigers, you could see the hurt and humiliation on their faces. To any other team, this may have been devastating for them. They had been knocked off of their throne, but this was Faye Baker's team. This team had been through so much hardship in the last year that nothing was going to hold them down. They weren't a team that buckled under pressure. So despite the fact that this team from Camden had came and beat them in their own gym and added insult to injury by slapping the floor, the girls walked out with their heads held high, determined to avenge their loss.

In the next two games the tigers defeated both teams and the following weekend, they once again met the Lady Wildcats in the first round of the playoffs at the Savannah Civic Center. Keeping in mind the girls had revenge on their minds; you won't be surprised to know that the Lady Tigers walked away with a 57-33 victory. And as the Lady Wildcats walked off the court, they were startled when the Tigers slapped the floor as if to say, "Now What?"

As the team continued with their season (eventually losing again to Camden County) in the playoffs, their coach continued to make strides in her therapy. The season ended with a record of 24-3, which is not too shabby for a coaching staff and team that should've received hazard pay for all the battles that they endured.

In the midst of it all, there "standing" head and shoulders above the rest was the 2001-2002 All Coastal Empire

Coach of the Year, Rhonda Faye Baker, a portrait in courage and dedication.

Never did she let this setback diminish her spirit. Not once did her conviction waver. She set a precedent that ultimately rubbed off on everyone around her. For four long years she has waged a battle for self-sufficiency and as each day passes, she is one step closer to reaching her goal.

Gone are the forearm crutches. In their place is a set of black canes. These, she began using at the end of the summer 2003, after a four week sojourn to Shepherd Center. Also gone are the days that Faye Baker has to wait on anyone to do the ordinary, everyday things. No longer is she required to have someone with her at all times. She can do just about anything she sets her mind to do. Some things she'll never do again, like running, playing softball, or basketball. She'll never be able to just turn around suddenly, compliments of the metal plate in her neck. She's adjusted to her lack of fine motor skills. "I don't have to ever do these things again," she reflects. "I just want to walk again," she repeats frequently.

For most of us, this is an ordinary, everyday thing, but for Faye, walking isn't just an ordinary thing. It is an *extraordinary* thing. Extraordinary because the doctors said she couldn't, but through God's grace, she is.

"No weapon formed against me shall prosper," Faye repeats the well-known Bible verse as she smiles the satisfied smile of someone who's been to the mountaintop.

Epilogue

December 9, 2004

*T*he night is quiet and still as the citizens of Liberty County come together for the first annual induction ceremony of the Athletic Hall of Fame. As Mr. Charles Shuman prepares to take the microphone and begin the ceremony, the "elite eighteen," (out of twenty inductees) mingle amongst each other and their guests.

Present for this night of champions are the who's who amongst Hinesville's best athletes and coaches as well as two at-large inductees. Comments such as "Look, there's Hokey Jackson and Delisha Milton," could be heard throughout the crowd. Guests and inductees alike marvel at meeting the infamous athletes of yesterday that they only heard or read about. Heads continuously turn and necks crane to catch a glimpse at the local celebrities, reporters and classmates that haven't been seen for years.

Sitting quietly among the crowd, Faye Baker looks on proudly as two of her brothers, Henry (HC), and Derrell are inducted for their past athletic accomplishments. As his best friend, Gary Gilliard surmises, Derrell is probably the third best athlete in his family, behind Barbara and Faye."

Listening as each brother thanked their parents for all

the love and unwavering support throughout their athletic careers, Faye reflects not only on growing up Baker, but most importantly on the latter years of her life.

Thinking about the last four years of her life, Faye is overcome with emotion for the couple that encouraged, nurtured, and comforted her during the hardest point in her life. A couple who unselfishly left the comfort of their home to move hundreds of miles away to live in a cramped hotel room for weeks strictly for the love of their child.

Contemplating how she made it thus far and how she has defied what the doctors told her four years ago while lying in the ICU ward of Memorial Hospital, Faye knows exactly what she needs to say to her parents, siblings and friends.

"And now, I would like to introduce you to your next Hall of Fame inductee, Rhonda Faye Baker." As she heard her name being announced, Faye quietly made her way to the podium to a huge round of applause.

"First of all, I would like to thank God for allowing me to be here amongst my family, friends and fellow inductees. As my brothers said, I have the best parents in the world. Throughout my childhood, they always found a way to be at all of my games. They somehow found a way to support five children equally throughout all of our endeavors, and even now, I can always look up in the stands when I'm coaching and find them there." Looking to the table on her left where her parents are seated along with her brother, Ronald, niece, Genese, and sister-in-law, Telli, Faye directs her comments there. "But mostly, I would like to thank my parents and my family for all of their support through the accident and my subsequent therapy. They have been there for me daily. So to my parents, my brothers and my sister, Barbara who couldn't be here tonight, I give this award back to you."

Glancing at the table in front of her, she said "And this is for my friends who have been there for me, I give this award back to you." Finishing off she said "and to God, I give all the glory." Wheeling away to a thunderous applause, Faye took her place at the end of the head table.

For Faye and the Baker family, this night proved to be one filled with accolades and pride. Pride in the accomplishments that the Baker children have made in the field of athletics, and accolades for the parents whose blessings helped make it all possible.

As the night draws to a close, and Faye in her state of euphoria, drifts into a blissful sleep, thoughts of her family usher her on this journey.

"Being faced with the knowledge that I was never supposed to walk again was the most devastating thing I ever had to deal with. But my family dared to say no. Not only did they tell me that I could overcome anything, they actively participated in helping me make it through. Even on those days that I just didn't feel like trying, I knew that my parents were going to walk through that door at lunchtime, rain or shine. I know it was grueling for them, but they never let me down, and I knew I couldn't let them down either. I know there are some good parents out there, but for me, mine are the best."

Smiling when she thinks of her big sister, Barbara, Faye ponders, "I wonder if she even knows how I watch and admire her. I watched her evolve from a fiery tempered young woman to a spiritual, God -filled woman. One day, I am going to be just like her."

On her brothers, Faye lovingly thinks, "Derrell made me tough. I would have never made it through without that mental and physical strength. Ronald is the smart, patient, even-tempered member that no family should be without." Laughingly, she remembers how Ron would drive her to school when she was in elementary school. She cringes when she recalls how she would sass Ronald when he asked her to hurry so he wouldn't be late for school. "He never fussed or yelled. He just patiently waited on me. And my oldest brother HC has been a Godsend. He devotes part of everyday to my therapy. Not once have I detected impatience or distraction. He has been committed to helping me walk and I can never repay him for that."

As Raymond Gross so eloquently put it, "Growing up in this area, you had to go the extra mile. Following in the footsteps of Derrell and HC Baker, you had to work hard to prove your worth. I was raised in an athletic family where there was none better, except maybe the Bakers. They are second to none."

One might never realize the double meaning this statement holds. Yes, when it comes to athletics, the Baker family is indeed second to none, but when it comes down to what really matters to Faye Baker; when the chips are down and your very survival counts on family strength, determination and devotion, the Baker family is indeed second to none.

And it's with this knowledge that Faye sleeps the contented rest of someone who has been truly blessed, and knows it.

A Gift For

_____

From

_____

Date

_____

Contents

Let cedar fill the air

With its spicy sweetness rare

Wake the carol—sound the chime—

Welcome! Merry Christmas time!

HELEN CHASE

Welcome Christmas Joy

We are joy seekers. We know that in everything, in every day, in every situation, if we just look under enough cushions and peek into enough corners, we will find joy. It's the shiny, childlike wonder that is found by those who actively seek it.

For a child at Christmastime, joy is seen in the reflection of lights, in the anticipation of brightly decorated gifts, in the glamour of "fancy" parties. As an adult, shopping, baking, and decorating can easily take over the season. With all the busyness, sometimes the true meaning of the season can get lost in the shuffle.

We can choose joy. It's always there, waiting to be discovered. In the delighted young eyes that discover baby Jesus in the manger for the first time. In the smiles around the table while decorating gingerbread angels. In the hymns we sing. In the knowledge that Christmas was motivated by the love of the One who created us.

As you read through *The Simple Joys of Christmas*, our prayer is that it will encourage you to celebrate the little joys as they come. That you will embrace the blessings of a season that celebrates the Creator in a manger. Immanuel, God with us. And that you will string together all the simple moments of Christmas joy into one continuous chain that will make this Christmas sweet and sacred.

the
simple joys
of
Christmas

Heartwarming Stories & Inspiration to Celebrate the Wonder of the Season

Ellie Claire
gift & paper expressions

...inspired by life

Ellie Claire™ Gift & Paper Corp.
Brentwood, TN 37027
EllieClaire.com

The Simple Joys of Christmas
© 2013 by Ellie Claire Gift & Paper Corp.
A Worthy Publishing Company

ISBN 978-1-60936-808-1

Stock or custom editions of Ellie Claire titles may be purchased in bulk for educational, business, ministry, fundraising, or sales promotional use. For information, please email info@EllieClaire.com.

Compiled by Jill Olson and Marilyn Jansen
Cover and interior design by ThinkPen | thinkpendesign.com
Typesetting by Kristin Chambers

1 2 3 4 5 6 7 8 9 – 18 17 16 15 14 13

Printed in China

"I go to church on the day itself," Donna explained, "but as for the rest of the celebration—"

"A Bob Hope Christmas," I mused. "Sounds like a great new tradition."

At this special time of year:
Follow the children.
Hear the joy in their laughter.
See the love in their eyes.
Feel the hope in their touch.

Do everything in love.

1 CORINTHIANS 16:14 NIV

We expect too much at Christmas. It's got to be magical. It's got to go right. Feasting. Fun. The perfect present. All that anticipation. Take it easy. Love's the thing. The rest is tinsel.

PAM BROWN

Homemade Happiness

My favorite...was a small picture framed with
construction paper, and reinforced with colored toothpicks....
"Do you like it?" asked the small giver excitedly.
"I used a hundred gallons of paste on it."
There were other gifts—the year of the bent coat hanger
adorned with twisted nose tissues and the year of the
matchbox covered with sewing scraps and fake pearls—
and then the small homemade gifts were no more.

I still receive gifts at Christmas. They are thoughtful.
They are wrapped with care. They are what I need.
But oh, how I wish I could bend low and receive a
gift of cardboard and library paste….

ERMA BOMBECK

START A HOMEMADE GIFT EXCHANGE TRADITION

A tradition of drawing family names for a homemade gift exchange can cause the creative wheels to turn. Items can be as simple as a photo album of your family's cell phone pictures from the year or a hand-carved keepsake box depending on age and skill. Other simple ideas:

1. Share a playlist from your music collection.
2. Popsicle stick puppets with a puppet show.
3. Hand knitted scarves or mittens.
4. A box of homemade all-occasion cards.
5. Jewelry made from beads and small charms with personal photos.
6. Natural air fresheners made from fruits, spices, and herbs.
7. Jars of cookie, brownie, or scone mixes.
8. Hand drawn certificates for services like lawn mowing or dishwashing.
9. Picture frames made from recycled materials: sticks, shells, greeting cards, etc.
10. Collect pinecones to make fire starters or scented pinecones.

A Mission of Tradition

BY JILL OLSON

*P*reparing the meal can be as much a part of a memory as the food itself. Why not gather family and friends together one day every Christmas season for a multi-generational time in the kitchen? Soak up generations of cooking tips from a grandmother, an aunt, or a sister-in-law—even if those beautiful women simply sit on a chair answering questions and retelling stories of when the recipes were made in years gone by.

Or create new traditions by embracing celebrations from other countries. Prepare and eat a meal from a country while learning about their native traditions. For example, in Mexico and many other Latin American countries, Santa Claus doesn't have the same visibility that he does in the United States. It is the three wise men who are the bearers of gifts, who leave presents in or near the shoes of children on Three Kings Day, as the wise men did for baby Jesus. It is celebrated January 6. So why not make burritos with your family or friends on that day while discussing the role of the wise men in the Christmas story?

14

TRADITIONAL CHRISTMAS TEA COOKIES

Make several batches so you can share with family and give as gifts.

Ingredients
- 1 cup butter
- 1 teaspoon vanilla extract
- 6 tablespoons powdered sugar
- 2 cups all-purpose flour
- 1 cup chopped pecans (or other nuts)
- 1/2 cup powdered sugar for decoration

Directions

Preheat oven to 350 degrees F (175 degrees C).

In a medium bowl, cream butter and vanilla until smooth. Combine the 6 tablespoons powdered sugar and flour; stir into the butter mixture until just blended. Mix in the chopped pecans. Roll dough into 1 inch balls, shape into crescent shapes, and place them 2 inches apart on an ungreased cookie sheet.

Bake for 12 minutes in the preheated oven. When cool, roll in remaining powdered sugar. Can be rolled in sugar a second time for a better coating.

Makes about 36 cookies.

Traditions. . .become something to look forward to, building a sense of security in our children that they'll want to pass on. When we carry them out, we put value on what is most important— time spent together, celebrating who we are.

BONNIE JENSEN

Where two or three are gathered together in my name, there am I in the midst of them.

MATTHEW 18:20 KJV

CHAPTER 2

The simple joy of Christmas Miracles

A life transformed by the power of God
is always a marvel and a miracle.

GERALDINE NICHOLAS

*"How will this be," Mary asked the angel,
"since I am a virgin?"*

LUKE 1:34 NIV

Christmas Will Find You

BY DEBRA S. BEHNKE

Now to him who is able to do immeasurably more than all
we ask or imagine, to him be glory!

EPHESIANS 3:20–21 NIV

Christmas Eve I woke up early for our big family dinner. I went to the kitchen to put in the turkey. But first I took a deep breath. I had a special Christmas request. A prayer not so much for me and our guests, but for my teenage son, Darryl. *Please, God, I asked, let us spend Christmas at home, and not in the hospital.*

Darryl was born with spina bifida and hydrocephalus. As an infant, he had a shunt implanted in his head to make it easier to drain the fluid that accumulated. Throughout his young life he visited the children's hospital regularly. Any day or night might include a surprise trip to the ER.

I don't want today ruined, I thought. *Darryl deserves a real Christmas more than any boy I know. Watching the Greenbay Packers play on television. Talking with Grandpa about the latest Nascar race. Teasing his younger sister, Marianne.* My prayer went on through several bastings of the turkey.

Our doorbell rang, and rang again. Everything was going perfectly. At dinner my father said grace. "Thank You, Lord, for filling this house with the Christmas spirit!" he said.

I looked over at Darryl. He was in trouble. The shunt was malfunctioning! Darryl passed out, his face falling forward on the table.

My father got him into the car and we raced to the hospital. The roads were empty. People were at home celebrating. *Why, Lord? Why today? Why can't Darryl have a real Christmas?*

In no time my son was prepped and in the operating theater, where doctors would repair the shunt. I sat in the waiting room. My parents and Marianne waited with me. We waited all night and into the morning. *Some Christmas,* I thought, flipping through a magazine.

Finally one of the nurses brought us good news. "Darryl's out of surgery, and he's just fine," she said.

I drove home to the empty house, showered, changed, and

drove back to the hospital. I didn't run into a single doctor or nurse on my way to Darryl's room. But when I got there a man was coming out. Not just any man—but Santa Claus himself.

"Merry Christmas," Santa bellowed in my face, and surprised me with a hug, his eyes sparkling with joy. His cheeks were rosy, his face vibrant, just like the Santas I remembered from childhood. Who was this Santa? In the hospital room I found Darryl and his sister sitting on the bed, surrounded by piles of shiny wrapping paper.

"Look what I got!" Marianne yelled, holding up a jewelry box. It was the exact jewelry box she had asked for, but I wasn't able to find. How did Santa get his hands on it? Darryl showed off a model of Dale Earnhardt's race car—his Nascar hero. And a Greenbay Packers sweatshirt, Darryl's favorite team. No one at the hospital could explain our strange but wonderful visit.

It wasn't the Christmas I'd prayed for. It was even better. It was the Christmas we would always remember. The Christmas that proved that wherever we are during the holiday season—in our homes surrounded by friends and family, or sitting in the hospital with a sick child—the spirit of Christ's love and mercy is always with us. No matter where we are, Christmas will always find us.

God, we thank you;
we thank you because you are near.
We tell about the miracles you do.

PSALM 75:1 NCV

I have called upon You, for You will hear me, O God;
Incline Your ear to me, and hear my speech.
Show Your marvelous lovingkindness by Your right hand,
O You who save those who trust in You

PSALM 17:6–7 NKJV

So thank GOD for his marvelous love, for his miracle
mercy to the children he loves; Offer thanksgiving
sacrifices, tell the world what he's done—sing it out!

PSALM 107:22 MSG

Let Christmas in its deepest magic possess your mind.
It will alter and stimulate everything about your observance
of the special season we now share. The Lord of Glory,
"endless, eternal and unchangeable in His being, wisdom,
power, and holiness," became man. Became a baby.

JACK HAYFORD

For unto us a Child is born,
Unto us a Son is given;
And the government will be upon His shoulder.
And His name will be called Wonderful, Counselor,
Mighty God, Everlasting Father, Prince of Peace.

ISAIAH 9:6 NKJV

The magical dust of Christmas glittered on the cheeks of humanity ever so briefly, reminding us of what is worth having and what we were intended to be.

MAX LUCADO

He does great things too marvelous to understand.

JOB 5:9 NLT

Something to Believe In

BY ANNE BENEDICT

Let the morning bring me word of your unfailing love.
PSALM 143:8 NIV

*I*t was after ten o'clock on Christmas Eve. My twin sister, Barbara, and I pressed our noses up to the big picture window in the living room.

"Mom and Dad have got to be home soon," Barbara said.

"Sure they will," I said. "Maybe they got held up in traffic." I didn't look Barbara in the eye. We were only ten, but this wasn't the first time we'd been left alone. Our parents were surely in a bar somewhere.

"I'm going to bed," I said finally. Barbara grabbed my arm. "Let's hang up our stockings," she said.

We rummaged around in Dad's dresser and pulled out his largest pair of socks. They looked sad hanging on the mantel. "When we wake up there will be lights and a tree, presents..." Barbara said dreamily.

"And Jimmy!" I said. Jimmy was our older brother and the one thing I could always believe in. Jimmy will make it feel like Christmas, I thought as I drifted off to sleep.

A loud noise woke me up. "What is it?" I whispered in the dark.

"Mom and Dad are home!" said Barbara. Hysterical sobs rang through the house. "How could you let this happen?" Mom screamed.

Our bedroom door burst open and Mom turned on the light. Her face was streaked with tears. Her words slurred. "There will be no Christmas in this house tomorrow. Just stay in bed."

Dad pushed his way in. "I picked up your gifts from layaway," he said…. "Someone broke into the car and stole everything! Even the tree tied to the roof!"

Even though it was after midnight, Mom called up Jimmy.

"So forget about Christmas this year," Mom said. "And one other thing: I'm leaving your father!"

"Mom's leaving?" Barbara said.

"What's going to happen to us?" I whispered.

A moment ago no Christmas seemed like the worst thing in the world. I thought about praying to God and telling him I just wanted my family back. But God was just another thing I couldn't believe in.

The next morning I woke up early. Barbara was already sitting up.

"We're not supposed to get out of bed," I mumbled.

"Well, I am," Barbara said. She climbed out of bed and put on her slippers. We crept to the bottom of the stairs and into the living room.

There stood a magnificent Christmas tree. Big glass balls hung from its branches and underneath were dozens of packages. Even the old socks on the mantel were stuffed with fruit.

We rushed up the stairs into our parents' room. "You were wrong!" Barbara yelled. Mom and Dad stumbled down the stairs, and stopped short when they saw the Christmas lights.

Barbara ripped the paper off the biggest box. "It's a farm set!" she shouted.

"I got a doll house!"

"It's beautiful, Anne," said Mom. She was sitting beside Dad on the couch. She reached for his hand!

As wonderful as the gifts were, they were all forgotten when we heard Jimmy at the front door. "Ho ho ho!" he called. Barbara and I pulled him into the living room. Jimmy looked at my parents in surprise. "I thought...?"

"We don't know," Mom said. She moved closer to Dad, and he put his arm around her.

"How could all these things just appear?" Dad said.

"Well, you know what they say," Jimmy said, with that chuckle I loved. "Christmas is a time for miracles."

Maybe God really did send angels to bring us our Christmas and answer the prayer I'd been afraid to make. Mom didn't leave Dad that day—or ever. Somehow that Christmas miracle was the push they needed to get help.

Over the years, I've retold the story to my children and their children.

"If Mom and Dad didn't do it, how did it happen?" I finally said to Jimmy years later during a visit. He chuckled, his face was lined now with age. "I guess I can tell you now," he said. "I went door-to-door in the middle of the night collecting decorations and presents people had to spare. I even found a tree in a vacant lot. Once I had everything I drove to the house. I pried open the basement window...."

"Why didn't you tell us it was you?" I asked, but I already knew. Jimmy wanted me to see there was something more to believe in. Jimmy gave us our Christmas, but God gave us our miracle.

Miracles remind us that God loves us and that on that first
Christmas so long ago He gave us the best present of all.
His love continues day by day—often through His
miracles…. Look around your life this Christmas.
Watch for the miracles of the season.

KAREN KINGSBURY

Give thanks to the LORD and pray to him.
Tell the nations what he has done.
Sing to him; sing praises to him.
Tell about all his miracles.
Be glad that you are his;
let those who seek the LORD be happy.
Depend on the LORD and his strength;
always go to him for help.
Remember the miracles he has done;
remember his wonders and his decisions.

PSALM 105:1–5 NCV

Not Such a Silent Night

BY VICKI POWELL

Make melody to Him…. Sing to Him a new song;
play skillfully with a shout of joy.
PSALM 33:2–3 NKJV

What a way to spend Christmas Eve: visiting my husband, Rick, who was stuck in the hospital with food poisoning. Two girls lugged a big black case onto the elevator with me—a harp! "We had a harpist at our wedding," I said.

"I'm playing for the patients tonight," one of them explained. The girls and I all got out on Rick's floor. "You go," Rick said sleepily when I told him about the harpist. "I don't have the energy."

I made my way to the gathering and heard the opening strains of "Silent Night." Suddenly I realized how blessed I was. I was healthy, Rick and I would go home tomorrow, and I was getting to hear my favorite hymn on my favorite instrument. All because two girls volunteered to give up their own Christmas Eve.

"I wish my husband could have made it out here to hear you," I said when the girls had finished. They winked at each other and dragged the harp into the hallway outside Rick's room to play "Silent Night."

CHAPTER 1

The simple joy of Christmas Traditions

The most vivid memories of Christmases past
are usually not of gifts given or received,
but of the spirit of love, the special warmth of
Christmas worship, the cherished little habits of the home,
the results of others acting in the spirit of Christ.

LOIS RAND

I commend you because you remember me
in everything and maintain the traditions just as
I handed them on to you.

1 CORINTHIANS 11:2 NRSV

Chain Reaction

BY CHERYL LAGLER

I have not stopped thanking God for you.

EPHESIANS 1:16 NLT

Remember the bright, festive construction-paper chains you used to make for your Christmas tree when you were a kid? My family puts a spiritual spin on this old-time tradition. Every year, we jot down the names of our loved ones or concerns on red and green strips of paper that we then make into a chain. The chain helps us count down the days of Christmas.

Starting December 1, we tear off a link and pray for whomever or whatever is written on the colored paper. It's a great way to remember to pray for those individuals and situations we might otherwise overlook. And it's exciting to see the chain grow shorter and shorter as Christmas draws near.

Many have forgotten the value and the meaning of traditions. They are the characteristics and activities which identify a family as unique and different.

DR. JAMES DOBSON

There is nothing quite so deeply satisfying as the
solidarity of a family united across the
generations and miles by a common faith and history.

SARA WENGER SHENK

Pray that we may be together soon.

HEBREWS 13:19 MSG

Therefore if you have any encouragement from being united
with Christ, if any comfort from his love, if any common
sharing in the Spirit, if any tenderness and compassion, then
make my joy complete by being like-minded, having the
same love, being one in spirit and of one mind. Do nothing
out of selfish ambition or vain conceit. Rather, in humility
value others above yourselves.

PHILIPPIANS 2:1–3 NIV

Angel of Nuremberg

BY JENNY WOOLF

Behold, I bring you good news of great joy which will be for all the people.
LUKE 2:10 NASB

Nuremberg, Germany, looks like an illustration for a fairy tale by the Brothers Grimm. A castle towers over the town. Steepled Gothic churches and ancient half-timbered houses line the River Pegnitz. The town's annual Christmas market, or Christkindlesmarkt, is the most colorful sight of all.

The big moment is the arrival of the Christkind, or Christ Child, represented by an angel with long golden curls and a tall crown. Her star-studded robes seem to defy the cold as she greets passersby with small gifts. Always portrayed by a teenage girl, the current Christkind is seventeen-year-old Eva Sattler.

The idea of the Christkind dates back to Martin Luther in the sixteenth century, but today's version has new meaning.

"During World War II," Eva explains, "old Nuremberg was reduced to rubble. Rebuilding the city seemed impossible." But the townsfolk did not abandon hope. They revived the traditional figure of the Christkind to symbolize their faith in the future.

Now, Nuremberg has been rebuilt almost as it was before. "The Christkind's message is always relevant," Eva says. "The angel is a symbol of love. Mingling with people, whoever they may be, she shows that the Christkind is there for them personally."

Eva was excused from school for the whole of December for a succession of twelve-hour days in which she visited hospitals, schools, shelters, and nursing homes. She gave television, radio, and press interviews. Like past Christkinder, she traveled all over the world. "It's tiring," Eva confesses, and stressful. "It's hard to see sickness and sadness. But I can help people by making them feel special."

All people will know that you are my
followers if you love each other.

JOHN 13:35 NCV

Simple Holiday
Food Traditions

Bring the joy of Christmas to the table with these tips.

1. Organize a cookie-baking party. Ask friends to bring their favorite holiday cookie, or the cookie dough to bake them together and sample each when they're still warm. Don't forget to print copies of the recipes.

2. Pick a meal for Christmas Eve (such as Chinese) and an entrée for Christmas Day (maybe ham or turkey), and have it every year. Or, choose a side dish that becomes the yearly tradition, even if it's just for laughs.

3. Make a holiday house with your family from gingerbread or graham crackers. If you don't claim culinary creativity, buy a set that has everything included.

4. Bake cookies or other goodies with your family and deliver them with your children to an elderly neighbor who lives alone, or to people who will be working through Christmas, such as your local fire station, police department, and hospital staff.

5. Volunteer family time at a soup kitchen or a food pantry, giving out food to people in need.

The generous will themselves be blessed.

PROVERBS 22:9 NIV

I don't like the turkey, but I like the bread he ate.

A THREE-YEAR-OLD'S REACTION TO HER CHRISTMAS DINNER

Love came down at Christmas,
Love all lovely, love divine;
Love was born at Christmas,
Star and angels gave the sign.

CHRISTINA ROSSETTI

A Bob Hope Christmas

BY LINDA NEUKRUG

*I pray that now at last by God's will the way may
be opened for me to come to you.*

ROMANS 1:10 NIV

I was perplexed when my friend Donna said to me, "My family's
going to have a 'Bob Hope Christmas' this year!"

"What on earth is a 'Bob Hope Christmas'?"

"You know how Bob Hope was always away from his family on Christmas,
entertaining the troops? Well, what about his own family celebration? When
did he do that?"

"I never really thought about that. Whenever he got back, I guess.
Whenever he could…"

"You see!" she said triumphantly. "That's a 'Bob Hope Christmas.' When
I first got married, there was so much hustle and bustle seeing both
families—each in a different city—that it took the joy out of celebrating. And
then after the kids came along, it became really hectic. Sometimes
we had to spend the whole day traveling. And we occasionally
had two turkey dinners!

"So I decided that when my kids had kids, we'd have a 'Bob
Hope Christmas.' It's important to their in-laws that the children
spend the twenty-fifth with them, so I tell my kids that
we'll do Christmas whenever it's convenient."

But you are…God's very own possession.
As a result, you can show others the goodness of God,
for he called you out of the darkness into his wonderful light.

1 PETER 2:9 NLT

Silent night, holy night,
Wondrous star lend thy light.
With the angels let us sing,
"Alleluia" to our King.
Christ the Savior is born,
Christ the Savior is born.

FRANZ GRUBER

HEADLINE OF HOPE

In Tennessee, two anonymous people paid the layaway bills for thirty families who were in danger of losing their items. Joyce, a recipient of the generosity, found out about the gift when she went to tell the manager that she was going to have to cancel her order.

He is your praise and he is your God, the one who has done mighty miracles you yourselves have seen.

DEUTERONOMY 10:21 TLB

CHAPTER 3

The simple joy of Christmas Surprises

Dear Lord, grant me the grace of wonder. Surprise me,
amaze me, awe me in every crevice of Your universe.
Delight me…. Each day enrapture me with
Your marvelous things without number.
I do not ask to see the reason for it all;
I ask only to share the wonder of it all.

ABRAHAM JOSHUA HESCHEL

"Look around at the nations;
look and be amazed!
For I am doing something in your own day,
something you wouldn't believe
even if someone told you about it."

HABAKKUK 1:5 NLT

Christmas Magic

BY KITTY MCCAFFREY

Sing to Him, sing praises to Him; speak of all His wonders.

1 CHRONICLES 16:9 NASB

Years had passed since I'd moved from North Carolina, but not a day went by that I didn't think of my old mountain home.

One holiday found me especially melancholy for the past. It was a few days before Christmas, and I hadn't so much as pulled the decorations out of the attic. My sons had sent me gifts, but I already knew what was wrapped up in those boxes. *Forgive me, Lord.* I've always loved the magic of Christmas. But there were no surprises for me this year.

A holiday display might help chase away the blahs. I decided to concentrate on the mantel. Maybe an angel or two. I certainly had plenty of those. My angel collection filled two lighted curio cabinets, mostly gifts over the years. Just looking at the figurines usually made me feel better.

Toward the back of one of the shelves, I spied a white bisque Madonna and Child. Where had that come from? For the life of me I couldn't remember.

Carefully I took the statue from the curio and brought it into the other room. I surrounded the Madonna and Child with red poinsettias, adding a white candle on either side. Simple and beautiful—but something was missing. Of course, I needed an angel! Not just any angel. It had to be the right one.

I scoured the shelves of my curio cabinets. The lights in the curios seemed to spotlight certain angels. "Pick me," they seemed to say, but I rejected them all. Won't anything work out for me this Christmas? Someone knocked on the front door. I was glad for the interruption.

I went to answer and saw the UPS man climbing into his truck. "Thank you," I called out. As I waved to him, I looked out at the scenery. The grass was green and the roses were still blooming. Not like the wintry Christmas landscape of my childhood.

I turned to go in and glanced at the return label on the package. It was from a cousin in snow-covered North Carolina! Suddenly I felt the warmth from every fireplace in my old mountain home. Inside I set the package on the living room table. Whatever was inside, it was the only surprise I had to look forward to on Christmas morning.

That night I couldn't sleep. I crawled out of bed and walked aimlessly through the house. There's no Christmas magic in here this year, that's for sure. Then the new package caught my eye. Why wait?

As the paper fell away, I couldn't believe my eyes.

An angel! Not just any angel, but a beautiful white bisque one exactly like I was looking for. I hopped to the task, filled with Christmas spirit. Who cared if it was the middle of the night? It was Christmas, after all! I redesigned the mantel display with the angel front and center. Magic! In the candlelight the faces of the figurines shone like heaven itself.

Thank You, Lord. Thank you, North Carolina. I settled in the recliner for the rest of the night, reveling in the wonder of Christmas—the very first one, and every one since.

The Lord will perfect that which concerns me;
Your mercy, O Lord, endures forever;
Do not forsake the works of Your hands.

PSALM 138:8 NKJV

Lord Jesus,
Master of both the Light and the darkness,
send Your Holy Spirit upon our preparations for Christmas.
We who have so much to do
seek quiet spaces to hear Your voice each day.
We who are anxious about many things
look forward to Your coming among us.
We who are blessed in so many ways
long for the complete joy of Your kingdom.
We whose hearts are heavy seek the joy of Your presence.
We are Your people, walking in darkness, yet seeking the light.
To You we say, "COME, LORD JESUS!"

HENRI J. M. NOUWEN

Jesus once again addressed them: "I am the world's Light.
No one who follows me stumbles around in the darkness.
I provide plenty of light to live in."

JOHN 8:12 MSG

Advent Defined

FROM DICTIONARY © 2005–2011 APPLE INC.

advent |'ad,vent|

noun [in sing.]
the arrival of a notable person, thing, or event: *the advent of television*.
• (Advent) the first season of the Christian church year, leading up to Christmas and including the four preceding Sundays.
• (Advent) Christian Theology the coming or second coming of Christ.
ORIGIN Old English, from Latin *adventus* 'arrival', from *advenire*, from *ad-* 'to' + *venire* 'come.'

I know the Messiah is coming—the one who is called Christ.
When he comes, he will explain everything to us.

JOHN 4:25 NLT

The origin of the Advent Calendar can be traced back to the mid-1800s, with the themes and constructions of calendars now varying widely. Each calendar day conceals a little surprise, from a beautiful miniature religious picture, to a little wooden toy or even a piece of candy. It is a great way to build daily anticipation (and patience) with little ones.

Advent calendars have been know to come in a variety of styles including a Countdown to Christmas with Kindness Calendar, where one act of random kindness is performed by one or more family members for each day, and recorded; and a Scripture advent, where different attributes of names of Jesus are referenced behind each window.

Advent is also meant...to refresh us and make us healthy, to be able to receive Christ in whatever form He may come to us.

MOTHER TERESA

Surprised by the Light

BY CATHY WALLACE

"Glory to God in the highest, and on earth peace, goodwill toward men!"
LUKE 2:14 NKJV

Our Christmas centerpiece was a tall golden candle, flanked by a pair of battery-powered ceramic angels that could light up. This year they didn't. At a past Christmas my sister had given one of them to my mother and one to me, but now that Mom had died both angels belonged to me.

I stood over the kitchen table, trying different combinations of batteries and wishing my mother were here for the holidays. Maybe it was appropriate that the angels remained dark. Eventually, I gave up and left them unlit.

Christmas morning I was the first one up and made my way into the kitchen. Something caught my eye. A small bright light. One angel, my mother's, had somehow come to life.

Merry Christmas, Mom, I thought. She was here with us for the holidays, after all.

Because of His boundless love, He became what we
are in order that He might make us what He is.

IRANAEUS

Life works most perfectly when a reciprocal love
relationship is in place between man and God.

BETH MOORE

If we love each other, God lives in us,
and his love is brought to full expression in us.

1 JOHN 4:12 NLT

There is no surprise more magical than the surprise of being loved.
It is the finger of God on [your] shoulder.

CHARLES MORGAN

God must have said, "I know what I'll do, I'll send my LOVE right
down there where they are. And I'll send it as a tiny baby, so they'll
have to touch it, and they'll have to hold it close."

GLORIA GAITHER

Today in the town of David a Savior has been born to you;
he is the Messiah, the Lord.

LUKE 2:11 NIV

Into all our lives, in many simple, familiar, homely ways,
God infuses this element of joy from the surprises of life,
which unexpectedly brighten our days, and fill our eyes with light.

SAMUEL LONGFELLOW

The precepts of the Lord are right,
giving joy to the heart.
The commands of the Lord are radiant,
giving light to the eyes.

PSALM 19:8 NIV

*Prayer…is an acknowledgment of our finitude, our
need, our openness to be changed, our readiness to be
surprised, yes astonished by the "beams of love."*

DOUGLAS STEERE

TEN CHRISTMAS SURPRISES FOR FAMILY OR FRIENDS

1. Prepare a picnic meal for your family or a time-strapped friend. Include their favorite foods, plates, silverware, dessert, and a note of love. It will bring a little bit of joy to the rush of the season.

2. Make a simple scrapbook or photo album. Grab photos from their Facebook wall or Instagram feed, cell phone, or digital camera and print them on photo paper. Put them in an album with a few comments on each page and you'll have a surprise they'll never forget.

3. Take time to get away for a few hours. Pick them up and go ice-skating, or shopping, or for a walk by the lake. Plan ahead and talk to bosses, family members, etc. to make it a surprise for only the recipient.

4. Give someone a day off from chores. Do the dishes, laundry, shoveling, or whatever is on their agenda for the day and let them catch their breath.

5. Make a book of coupons for services you will do after the holidays like putting away the decorations, testing lights, or vacuuming up tree needles. Be creative and include things that are typically not your responsibility.

6. Create an individual ornament for everyone in your family or group of friends using decorated cookies, craft paint on glass bulbs, or a permanent marker and pinecones. Include their name and the year and use it as a gift decoration or place setting.

7. Be sentimental. Write a poem, sing a song, or make a photo collage that depicts how special they are to you. Be it ever so humble, there is nothing like a gift straight from the heart.

8. Surprise them with an impromptu late-night drive around the best-decorated neighborhoods. Make it even more fun by wearing pajamas and taking along thermoses of hot chocolate.

9. Use big cookie cutters to cut bread into holiday shapes for sandwiches. Then pack fun lunches for everyone to take on an outing to feed the ducks, select a Christmas tree, or visit a friend whose relatives live far away.

10. Attend a Christmas concert or a local production of one of the holiday plays like *The Nutcracker* or *A Christmas Carol*.

The coming of Christ by way of a Bethlehem manger
seems strange and stunning. But when we take him out of
the manger and invite him into our hearts, then the meaning
unfolds and the strangeness vanishes.

NEIL C. STRAIT

If anyone is in Christ, the new creation has come:
The old has gone, the new is here!

2 CORINTHIANS 5:17 NIV

All heroes are shadows of Christ.

JOHN PIPER

How silently,
How silently the wondrous gift is given.
So God imparts to human hearts
The wonders of His heaven.

PHILLIPS BROOKS

CHAPTER 4

The simple joy of a Family Christmas

Looking back on all that we've shared and all that is yet to come,
I realize that nothing life may offer me could make me happier
than a future filled with loving my family.

*I have no greater joy than to hear that
my children are walking in the truth.*

3 JOHN 1:4 NIV

A Hidden Glory

BY GAIL THORELL SCHILLING

Yet I am not alone....

JOHN 16:32 NIV

n 1996 my daughter Tess, seventeen, was about one thousand miles away for Christmas. She couldn't come home. Then, she injured her knee. She called crying on Christmas morning.

"Oh, honey, I wish you could be here too. Did you like your presents?"

"No. I'm too depressed to open them."

"Well..." How to comfort long-distance? "You aren't alone now! We're here. Kids, get on the bedroom phone. Tess is going to open her gifts!"

First she opened the red fleece cloche hat and mittens. "So soft. They fit great, Mom."

Then the surfboard-shaped pillow her brother had sewn in home economics class. "You really did this? Way to go, Tom!" Now there was energy in her voice.

Next, slippers. The harp tape. "I love them!"

Sounds of paper tearing. "What are you opening now, honey?"

"A book—must be from Mom!"

A squeal. "Now what?"

"Peppermint patties, pinwheel cookies, and fudge!"

Finally a soft "wow" as she found her Christmas card and check to buy the coat she had admired. Her dismal mood had vanished.

Every heart comes home for Christmas.

If your gift is to encourage others, be encouraging.
If it is giving, give generously.... And if you have a gift for
showing kindness to others, do it gladly.

ROMANS 12:8 NLT

O come, O come, Emmanuel
And ransom captive Israel
That mourns in lonely exile here
Until the Son of God appear
Rejoice! Rejoice! Emmanuel
Shall come to thee, O Israel.

One Christmas when this hymn came on the radio, I asked my children if they knew what the words meant. I turned it up, they listened. No one had an answer. That led to a discussion starting with what Emmanuel means, who and what Israel referred to, what exile meant, and what was the reason for rejoicing. It was a little quieter in the car when that song came on the next time as my children thought about its meaning.

JILL OLSON

My Christmas Star

BY FRANCES MCGEE-CROMARTIE

Each part does its own special work…so that the whole body
is healthy and growing and full of love.

EPHESIANS 4:16 NLT

My husband, Michael, and I squeezed into our seats at St. Rita's School just before the start of the annual Advent program. My daughter Elizabeth would be spending the evening hidden among the bell choir and the chorus.

She'd been a mystery to me since she hit her teens. Why was she so reluctant to share her talents? Didn't she realize how important leadership skills are? Some younger kids took the stage. I remembered when Elizabeth was that age, how she burst out in song at the least provocation.

One of the little girls read a short verse. Her beaming mother popped up to snap her picture. I wanted to be that mother again, Elizabeth to be that child. I praised her. Encouraged her. Asked her about school. Her responses rarely went beyond "Everything's fine, Mom."

God, I'm not sure I even know who my daughter is anymore.

The bell choir took the stage. I strained to see Elizabeth. Between numbers, a young man read about the shepherds. The woman behind me leaned forward with her camera. Next up was the chorus.

The audience's eyes were glued to the soloists. It felt as if every eighth grader had at least one starring moment. Everyone except my daughter.

The show ended to thunderous applause. I looked for the nearest exit but the aisles were already clogged. The woman behind me smiled. "Wasn't the program wonderful?" she asked…. "What's your child's name?"

"Our daughter is Elizabeth…"

"Elizabeth? You're Elizabeth's mom?" the woman said, her eyes wide with excitement. "My son talks about her all the time."

I searched my memory to recall the names of any boys my daughter had mentioned. I looked to Michael. He only shrugged. Could she be thinking of a different Elizabeth?

"She's always so kind to him," the other mom continued. "She's really helped him fit in."

"Oh," I said, finally understanding. "It's your first year. Welcome to St. Rita's. Last year Elizabeth was new. I'm sure she understands what it's like."

"No, that's not it," she said quietly. "My son is autistic. This year has been a positive experience because of Elizabeth. She's made a difference in how others see him. I'd really like to meet her."

I saw Elizabeth waiting at the door of her classroom, her face unreadable as usual. I turned to the woman and quickly introduced her to Elizabeth. I could hardly believe the change that came over my daughter.

"Hello," Elizabeth said. She smiled, stood up straight, and made eye contact. "I like your son. He's got a great sense of humor. Sometimes he and I are the only ones who get the teacher's jokes." Then she hooked her arm in Michael's and tugged him down the hall. I turned to the woman, whose face was bright with happiness.

"You've got a good kid there," she said. "She's something special."

"Thanks," I said, nodding, slowly. "She really is."

Interpersonal skills and the ability to see others' God-given talents, weren't those the hallmarks of a good leader too? I wished the other mom a Merry Christmas and hurried to catch up to my husband and my daughter, my own shining star.

Let this Christmas season be a renewing of the mind of Christ in our thinking, and a cleansing of our lives by His pure presence. Let His joy come to our weary world through us.

GERALD KENNEDY

Other things may change us,
but we start and end with family.

ANTHONY BRANDT

Heavenly Father, my prayer to You today is one of
thanksgiving, gratitude, and praise. Thank You so
much for Your favor and marvelous generosity to my
family and me. Every good and perfect gift truly comes
directly from Your hand to us through Your giving
heart of kindness and love. I cannot begin to express
to You how greatly blessed and grateful I am for the
gift of my children. I do, with all my heart, receive each
life that has come into our family as Your beautiful
gift. I cannot find the words to thank You enough.

ROY LESSIN

You don't choose your family.
They are God's gift to you,
as you are to them.

DESMOND M. TUTU

God decided in advance to adopt us into his own family by bringing us to himself through Jesus Christ. This is what he wanted to do, and it gave him great pleasure.

EPHESIANS 1:5 NLT

WE'RE-ALL-IN-THIS-TOGETHER NUT CLUSTERS

This treat is a lot like many families—a little nutty, a little sweet, and all stuck together.

Ingredients

1 24-ounce package of chocolate almond bark
1 24-ounce package of chocolate chips
2 pounds of salted peanuts (or pecans or walnuts or macadamia nuts)

Directions

Line two large cookie sheets with waxed paper.
In a microwave-safe bowl, melt chocolate, 30 seconds at a time until it is mostly melted. Remove from microwave and stir until the lumps are gone. Quickly add the nuts. Stir until coated.
Drop by spoonful onto waxed paper. Let harden in cool area for 15–30 minutes.

Though I have seen the oceans and mountains, though I have read great books and seen great works of art, though I have heard symphonies and tasted the best wines and foods, there is nothing greater or more beautiful than those people I love.

CHRISTOPHER DE VINCK

Room at the Inn?

BY LINDA BREEDEN

Live deeply in Christ. Then we'll be ready for him when he appears,
ready to receive him with open arms.

1 JOHN 2:28 MSG

It seemed like a great idea for our church to put the youth group in charge of the annual Christmas pageant—until they asked my son, Charlie, to take part in it.

"Please let him be in the Christmas play," begged Julie, the teenaged head of the youth group, when she cornered my family after church.

"Charlie just turned four," I said. "That's too young to be in a play."

"But we really want him to be the innkeeper," she said. "He would only have one line. We know he can do it. Don't we, everybody?" She turned to the crowd of young people hanging back in the foyer. They answered with a chorus of "Yes!" and "Charlie can do it!" and "Please, Mrs. Breeden?"

Charlie didn't seem to understand what was going on, but he liked people shouting his name. My husband, Frank, shrugged. How could we disappoint the kids?

"As long as it's one line," I said.

Julie swept Charlie up. "We can do it! We can do it!"

"Are you sure?" Frank asked.

"Nope," I said. "I'm not." But I couldn't blame the kids for thinking Charlie was a natural. He did speak very well for his age, and he was already a hit with his James Cagney impressions. Still, going onstage was a big experience for a four-year-old. And I wondered if the innkeeper might wind up sounding like Cagney!

Charlie enjoyed the play practices.

The closer we got to opening night, the more I worried. We practiced and practiced.

On opening night Charlie showed signs of a cold. "Do you want to take him out of the play?" Frank said as we prepared to leave for the performance.

"I do," I admitted. "But we can't back out now. You can't have a Christmas pageant without an innkeeper."

Everyone is depending on him, I thought as I dressed Charlie in his flannel bathrobe and draped a towel over his head, secured with a safety pin. That's not fair to a four-year-old.

When we got to the church, Julie and the older kids whisked him away behind the curtain.

Finally the lights dimmed and the curtains opened. In the center stood Charlie. His lower lip was puckering, and I thought he might cry as he searched the audience.

I'm right here, Charlie, I thought, sliding to the edge of my seat. Only Frank's hand on my shoulder kept me from jumping up on the stage.

"I am Joseph from Galilee," announced twelve-year-old Jason. "My wife is heavy with child and we have traveled a long way these past days. We are weary and need a room."

Jason turned to the tiny innkeeper, waiting for his answer. Charlie looked a bit startled, then dazed. Once again he searched the audience. I gripped Frank's hand and whispered, *"Please, Jesus, be with Charlie onstage. He needs your help!"*

Jason turned to Charlie again. "Innkeeper," he said, obviously trying to nudge him into remembering. "Innkeeper, do you have a room for us?"

Charlie suddenly snapped to attention. He looked around the stage, and I could see he was taking it all in. He stood up straight and considered the weary travelers. Mary, who couldn't quite conceal her "heaviness," and Joseph, so tall and protective. Charlie looked up at him. That's my boy…. Now say your line, Charlie. Go on, you can do it. The audience waited. Everyone was rooting for Charlie.

"Y'all come on in!" he sang out. "I gots room for Baby Jesus."

For a moment nobody made a sound. Then heads swiveled to me and Frank, the parents of the wayward pageant actor. I told them he was too young, I thought. Now I'd embarrassed everyone.

From the back of the audience, a woman called out, "Amen, child." She was answered by a chorus of amens throughout the church.

The quick-thinking Joseph didn't take the innkeeper up on his offer. He chose a bed in the manger instead. But Charlie stood proud in his bathrobe throughout the rest of the play.

Afterward, the older kids and all the parents congratulated Frank and me, and our adorable innkeeper who had room for Baby Jesus. Wasn't that what Christmas was all about? I had asked Jesus to be with Charlie onstage that night. But Jesus had found an even more loving spot in Charlie's heart.

Mary treasured up all these things and pondered them in her heart. The shepherds returned, glorifying and praising God for all the things they had heard and seen, which were just as they had been told.

LUKE 2:19–20 NIV

All the great purposes of God culminate in Him.
The greatest and most momentous fact which the history
of the world records is the fact of His birth.

CHARLES H. SPURGEON

CHAPTER 5

The simple joy of Christmas Angels

An angel announced His conception and gave Him His name.
The heavenly host sang a glorious anthem at His birth.
By the extraordinary star, the very heavens indicated His coming....
He was the most illustrious child ever born—the holy child of Mary,
the divine Son of God.

BILLY GRAHAM

*An angel of the Lord appeared to him in a dream and said...
"She will give birth to a son, and you are to give him the name Jesus."*

MATTHEW 1:20–21 NIV

Friendly Skies

BY LINDA PASSARELLI

*I love the LORD because he hears my voice and
my prayer for mercy. Because he bends down to listen,
I will pray as long as I have breath!*

PSALM 116:1–2 NLT

Two weeks before Christmas our house was burglarized. It was a blessing that our eleven-year-old was away visiting family, but I cried when the flight attendant released her to me at the airport. "Moriah," I said. "Your Christmas presents were stolen, honey." Her father and I couldn't afford to replace them. Moriah said she was just glad we were okay. Still, I could hear disappointment in her voice. Lord, save Christmas for Moriah.

A few days later the phone rang. "I'm calling from the airline," the woman said. "Please tell Moriah that there's a package on its way from the North Pole."

"I don't understand."

"I'm Chanda. I was Moriah's flight attendant and overheard you at the airport. Moriah's a delightful girl. She will have presents this Christmas."

Moriah's eyes were big as saucers as she opened her gifts. There was even one for me. The flight attendant wasn't just Santa's helper. She was a Christmas angel.

PASTA ANGELS ACTIVITY

These dainty little angels are adorable and easy to make. The leftover pasta can go right into the cupboard for quick meals during the holidays. If small children are included, use craft glue instead of hot glue.

Supplies:

    20 mm wooden bead, for the head

    Pasta: Rigatoni (tubes), for the dress

                Rotelle (wagon wheels), for the collar

                Farfalle (bow-tie), for the wings

                Elbow macaroni for the arms

                Ditalini (little tubes), for hair

                Stelline (stars), for decoration, optional

    Spray Paint

    Fine-tip permanent marker

    Ribbon for hanging

Hot-glue the wagon wheel (spokes down) to the top of the rigatoni. (It should look like a big cap on a bottle.) Then glue the head bead on top of the wagon wheel. Glue the bow-tie to the back of the rigatoni just below the wagon wheel collar. For arms, glue one elbow macaroni on each side of the dress, under the collar. For the hair, glue a row of Ditalini around the bead, from one side of the collar to the other. Then fill in the back of the head bead with the more Ditalini. Decorate the front of the collar and the bottom of the dress with stars (optional).

    Rest angels on top of pencils stuck through empty cereal boxes or Styrofoam cups. Choose the color and finish of spray paint desired. Three coats will be needed, with drying between coats.

    When completely dry, draw on a face with the marker. Insert ribbon through top noodle to hang.

Suddenly a great company of the heavenly host appeared
with the angel, praising God and saying, "Glory to God in the
highest heaven, and on earth peace to those on whom his favor
rests. When the angels had left them and gone into heaven, the
shepherds said to one another, "Let's go to Bethlehem and see this
thing that has happened, which the Lord has told us about."

LUKE 2:13–15 NIV

Off to one side sits a group of shepherds. They sit silently on the
floor, perhaps perplexed, perhaps in awe, no doubt in amazement.
Their night watch had been interrupted by an explosion of light
from heaven and a symphony of angels. God goes to those who
have time to hear Him—and so on this cloudless night
He went to simple shepherds.

MAX LUCADO

The Night of the Christmas Nurse

BY KAREN TRACY

For the LORD is good and his love endures forever;
his faithfulness continues through all generations.

PSALM 100:5 NIV

*E*mergency medicine doesn't take holidays off, but this was the first time I'd pulled an EMT shift on Christmas. Already we were racing to a studio apartment in an independent living community to answer the night's first 911 call. I couldn't help thinking this was supposed to be a night of miracles, not injuries.

The ambulance had barely come to a full stop when my partner, Dan, and I jumped out with a gurney. A staff member from the facility waited at the apartment door. "Miss Lily had a fall," she said as we knelt down around the elderly, white-haired woman on the floor. "She's one hundred years old," the staff member informed us with a note of pride.

"We're going to examine you to see where you're hurt," I told her. Miss Lily nodded. She winced when Dan touched her hip but tried to hide it behind a smile.

"Shortening and rotation of the leg and foot on the affected side," Dan said. Miss Lily winced again. "Increased pain with palpitation to the hip." Dan and I nodded to each other. It was a classic case of fractured hip—very common in elderly people. We lifted her gingerly onto the gurney, started her IV in the ambulance and headed to the High Desert Medical Center at full speed.

I knew the harsh realities of a broken hip. Many older patients never fully recover their strength or stop hurting from their injury. We learned that Miss Lily had been relatively pain-free and strong for 100 years. Even now she bravely chatted with us between gasps of pain.

Once we got her settled in a hospital bed in the ER, Miss Lily shut her eyes, signaling she was finally overwhelmed by the pain. She looked gray and wilted on the bright white hospital sheets. Colleen, one of the nurses, hooked her up to a cardiac monitor. She pulled the curtain shut around Miss Lily for privacy.

It was Christmas somewhere, but in the ER it looked like any night. I got out of the way and went to the supply closet to restock the ambulance. Afterward I glanced in at Miss Lily. She lay propped up on some pillows, eyes closed, breathing unevenly. *She might not make it through the night*, I thought. It still didn't seem right. Christmas was a time of surprises and miracles, not suffering and death.

I sat down outside the ER to catch up on my paperwork. When I looked up from my writing I saw Dan pushing the gurney away from Miss Lily's area. I went to help.

Just then Colleen popped her head out from behind Miss Lily's curtain. She looked stunned. "What is it?" I asked. ER nurses have seen it all. What was it that had left Colleen speechless? Instead of answering me, Colleen drew back the curtain. Miss Lily sat there, upright in her bed, beaming.

"Miss Lily," I stammered, "you look much better." Her cheeks were all apples and peaches as she nodded. "Yes, yes," she said. "The medicine worked wonders, just wonders!"

As far as I knew no one had administered any medications to Miss Lily. Colleen confirmed my impression with a shake of her head.

"Which medicine?" I asked.

"Why, the little pill the nurse gave me," she said. "The nice nurse with the white cap." White cap? Nurses hadn't worn them in decades. My own sister, an RN, had complained about having to wear one for her formal graduation photo. No nurse would bother with a cap while on duty—especially in the ER. And besides, no one would have given Miss Lily any pills. Any medicine would have been administered through the IV in her arm.

But there didn't seem any reason to tell Miss Lily any of that. Instead I just squeezed her hand gently. "Merry Christmas," I said.

A thrill of hope the weary world rejoices
For yonder breaks a new and glorious morn.
Fall on your knees! O, hear the angel voices!
O night divine, O night when Christ was born.

PLACIDE CAPPEAU

You don't need candlelight and fireside glow to make Christmas happen. Trees, ornaments, gifts, and all of it are splendid embellishments. Not necessary, but so very nice. It's Him. He's finding more and more opened inns these days. It's priceless to discover the pleasure of His company.... May your home know something of all this glory during these days.

JACK HAYFORD

Good news from heaven the angels bring;
glad tidings to the earth they sing:
To us this day a child is given,
To crown us with the joy of heaven.

MARTIN LUTHER

ANGEL FOOD CANDY

The delicious crunchy candy, a tradition in many families, can be made fresh in your own kitchen.

Ingredients:
- 1 cup white sugar
- 1 cup dark corn syrup
- 1 tablespoon vinegar
- 1 tablespoon baking soda
- 1 pound chocolate coating or almond bark

Directions

Grease a 9x13-inch baking pan.

In a saucepan over medium heat, combine sugar, corn syrup, and vinegar. Stir until sugar dissolves. Heat, without stirring, to 300 to 310 degrees F (149 to 154 degrees C), or until a small amount of syrup dropped into cold water forms hard, brittle threads. Remove from heat and carefully stir in baking soda. Pour into prepared pan; do not spread. (Batter will not fill pan.) Allow to cool completely. Break cooled candy into bite sized pieces.

In the microwave or over a double boiler, melt coating chocolate, stirring frequently until smooth. Be careful not to overcook chocolate. Dip candy pieces into melted chocolate coating. Let set on waxed paper until chocolate hardens. Store tightly covered.

Guide in the Storm

BY LYN THOMPSON

For such is God,
our God forever and ever;
He will guide us until death.

PSALM 48:14 NASB

My windshield wipers barely worked. The wind was raging. I was used to harsh German winters in the two years since my husband had been stationed at the U.S. Air Force base, but this storm was a nightmare. Ken was home with our two sick children. Our nine-year-old and I were driving back after attending Christmas services.

"Mommy!" said Krista. "How will we make it home?"

"Pray," I told her. Krista bowed her head.

We reached the hilltop on the road that led to the village where we lived. No streetlamps. Only my headlights pierced the darkness. How would I get down that icy hill?

"Look!" Krista shouted. A car sat by the side of the road. A young man was in the driver's seat with the window down.

"Do you need help?" I asked, pulling alongside him.

"No, ma'am," he said, "but you'll never make it home unless you follow me." He pulled his car in front of ours. Ever so slowly we made it safely down the hill. I patted Krista's hand. When I looked at the road again, the car was gone. No disappearing taillights, no noise, nothing. Thanks to a child's prayer, an angel had been waiting for us.

Don't worry about anything; instead, pray about everything; tell God your needs and don't forget to thank him for his answers.

PHILIPPIANS 4:6 TLB

"Gloria, Gloria!" they cry, for their song embraces
all that the Lord has begun this day:
Glory to God in the highest of heavens!
And peace to the people with whom He is pleased!

WALTER WANGERIN JR.

"Peace on earth, and mercy mild,
God and sinners reconciled!"
Joyful all ye nations, rise,
Join the triumph of the skies;
With th' angelic host proclaim,
"Christ is born in Bethlehem!"

CHARLES WESLEY

*All heaven will praise your great wonders, LORD;
myriads of angels will praise you
for your faithfulness.*

PSALM 89:5 NLT

CHAPTER 6

The *simple joy* of Christmas Giving

For somehow, not only at Christmas,
but all the long year through,
the joy that you give to others
is the joy that comes back to you.

JOHN GREENLEAF WHITTIER

Give away your life; you'll find life given back,
but not merely given back—given back with bonus and blessing.
Giving, not getting, is the way. Generosity begets generosity.

LUKE 6:38 MSG

Ready to Roll

BY ASHLEY DEVECHT

We are to God the pleasing aroma of Christ.

2 CORINTHIANS 2:15 NIV

Some families debate about the best time to open presents—Christmas Eve or Christmas morning. When I was growing up there was no question—the night before Christmas, because Christmas morning we were way too busy. The thing I remember best about those mornings is the aroma of oven-fresh cinnamon rolls.

It all started before I was born. My mom had just graduated college and married my dad. She'd heard that the local Meals on Wheels volunteers had Christmas off. She was familiar with the program because of what they'd done for her mom, my grandma Evie. Not only did they deliver a hot meal every day, they provided good company. Mom hated to think of the elderly and the sick going hungry for a day.

"Not everyone has somewhere to go," she told the Meals on Wheels folks. "Let me handle Christmas." She and Dad had only one small oven in their duplex. They used it for the potatoes and green beans, and put the hams out on the grill on their back deck, no small feat considering that they lived in Michigan!

First she cooked and delivered just a handful of meals, but her list of customers got longer. She asked friends from church and Bible study for help. They were glad to pitch in. Drivers were harder to find. Enter the cinnamon rolls.

See, Mom is known for her kitchen magic, especially when it comes to baking, and she's not above using food as a bribe. Once, Dad threw his back out and Mom baked a batch of double-chocolate brownies to get the neighbor boys to mow the lawn. My uncles and grandpa—all of them engineers—were induced to put a new deck on our house with the promise of Mom's mint-Oreo-fudge ice-cream cake. What could she make to lure drivers for Christmas Day? Sweet, buttery, melt-in-your-mouth cinnamon rolls, that's what.

Those Christmas mornings our house was like a beehive. I scurried into the kitchen to find the famous rolls kept warm under towels. There were plates and plates of them. "Put them out," Mom said. "The drivers will be here any minute."

In a way, the drivers were our Santas. There was Bruce, tall and lanky, giving us big hugs. He ducked coming into the kitchen, his head almost skimming the top of the door frame. And Jack, who was short and bald, would pick up a cinnamon roll and divide it in half for my sister and me. "Merry Christmas," he'd declare. Paul, one of Mom and Dad's friends from church, loved driving so much he eventually volunteered for Meals on Wheels year round.

They ate their rolls, got their delivery routes and loaded up their meals, making sure to start out early so they'd have enough time to visit with their customers.

Friends are surprised when I tell them how I spent Christmas mornings as a kid. No sleeping in, no mad scramble for presents under the tree. Just the aroma of Mom's cinnamon rolls, and the even warmer sense of her generosity.

*It is Christmas in the heart that
puts Christmas in the air.*

W. T. ELLIS

I love the Christmas-tide, and yet
I notice this, each year I live;
I always like the gifts I get,
But how I love the gifts I give!

CAROLYN WELLS

Christmas, my child, is love in action.... When you love
someone, you give to them, as God gives to us. The greatest gift
He ever gave was the person of His Son, sent to us in human
form so that we might know what God the Father is really like!
Every time we love, every time we give, it's Christmas.

DALE EVANS ROGERS

The Blessing of Time

BY DEBBIE MACOMBER

Let us not love with word or with tongue,
but in deed and truth.

1 JOHN 3:18 NASB

While my boys were in college, they struggled with what to buy their grandparents for Christmas. They wanted my mom and dad to know how much they loved them, but finding a gift within their price range became more of a challenge each year.

Then one Thanksgiving, my father casually mentioned how much he had loved decorating the house with lights every Christmas. He couldn't any longer and that saddened him.

Shortly afterward, Ted and Dale came to me with an idea. As their Christmas gift to their grandparents, they wanted to make the three-hour drive to their house and decorate it for Christmas.

I pitched in and purchased the necessary supplies, and the boys spent two days stringing up lights and boughs all around the outside of the house. Every bush, plant, and tree trunk was wrapped in lights. My dad beamed with pride that his house was the most brilliantly lit home in the neighborhood.

Ted and Dale had such a good time with my parents, and each other, that they returned every couple of months and completed necessary tasks around the house that my father could no longer manage. My parents treasured this special gift more than anything the boys could have purchased.

I learned something valuable from my sons that year: An extra toy under the tree for the grandchildren won't mean half as much as playing a game with them or holding a special tea party complete with fancy hats and gloves. The gift of my time will be remembered long after they have outgrown their toys.

How beautiful is an open hand that will give without a moment's hesitation…and oh, how God's love can be seen in the palm of it.

Give, and it will be given to you. A good measure, pressed down, shaken together and running over, will be poured into your lap. For with the measure you use, it will be measured to you.

LUKE 6:38 NIV

SIMPLE WAYS TO GIVE YOUR TIME

1. Adopt a family either in your area or through a Christmas outreach organization. Involve the whole family in purchasing, packaging, and delivering the gifts.
2. Make a meal for a family in need or a senior citizen who cannot get out and deliver it with fanfare. Include a centerpiece, plates, and drinks.
3. Bake cookies, low calorie snacks, or whatever is appropriate for your neighbors and wrap them with care. Deliver with an invitation to church for Christmas services.
4. Deliver treats to people who have to work on Christmas Eve or Christmas. Taking time out of your day to make the trip will be worth it.
5. Clean house for your parents, friends, or family members the week before Christmas so they can have time to refresh or decorate or bake.
6. Drive a needy person to church, the grocery store, or the post office. There are so many errands around the holidays and those who have difficulty driving will appreciate the help.
7. Take an hour to sing Christmas carols to neighbors, senior citizens, prisoners, home-bound, or homeless people.
8. Have your family collect donations from the neighbors, family, or church members to donate to holiday food drives. It doesn't take long and is needed in almost every community at Christmas time.
9. Volunteer to help make home repairs, do mending, grocery shop, or put up Christmas decorations for people who cannot do it themselves.
10. Give blood. It takes so little time and gives life to so many.

How will you your Christmas keep?
Feasting, fasting, or asleep?
...Be it kept with joy or pray'r,
Keep of either some to spare;
Whatsoever brings the day,
Do not keep but give away.

ELEANOR FARJEON

The joy of receiving is in far more than the gifts—
that when we receive graciously and gladly,
we reciprocate the gift with joy and gratitude;
and in that moment of shared happiness and understanding,
giver and receiver "connect."

JENNY WALTON

GINGERBREAD COOKIE MIX IN A JAR

Put the ingredients in a jar, tie a bow around it, and you have a great gift to give a hostess, friend, or co-worker.

Ingredients

3 ½ cups all-purpose flour

1 teaspoon baking powder

1 teaspoon baking soda

2 teaspoons ground ginger

1 teaspoon ground cloves

1 teaspoon cinnamon

1 teaspoon ground allspice

1 cup packed brown sugar

(Additional ingredients needed to
    bake cookies. See below)

Directions

Mix 2 cups of the flour with the baking soda and baking powder. Mix the remaining 1 1/2 cups flour with the ginger, cloves, cinnamon, and allspice. In a 1 quart, wide mouth canning jar, layer the ingredients starting with the flour and baking powder mixture, then the brown sugar, and finally the flour and spice mixture. Pack firmly between layers.

Place a circle of gingerbread fabric between lid and ring and tie a gingerbread man cookie cutter onto jar with ribbon!

Attach a card to the jar with the following directions:

Preheat oven to 350 degrees F (175 degrees C). • Empty contents of jar into a large mixing bowl. Stir to blend together. Mix in 1/2 cup softened butter or margarine, 3/4 cup molasses, and 1 slightly beaten egg. Dough will be very stiff, so you may need to use your hands. Cover, and refrigerate for 1 hour. • Roll dough to 1/4 inch thick on a lightly floured surface. Cut into shapes with a cookie cutter. Place cookies on a lightly greased cookie sheet about 2 inches apart. • Bake for 10 to 12 minutes in preheated oven. When completely cool, decorate as desired (or top with honey and eat when they are hot out of the oven!)

HOW TO BE A FAMILY OF GIVERS IN A SEASON OF GETTING

- As a family divide, your money into giving, saving, spending, and investing. Involve all family members and discuss expectations.
- As a family, develop weekly, monthly, and yearly budgets and document them. Discuss the possibility of using money from Christmas gifts to increase giving to your budget.
- Have discussions about the charities, groups, or missions your family wants to support during the holidays. Research relief, missions, and humanitarian organizations to find the ones that fit your lifestyle and beliefs.
- Develop realistic personal giving goals for each person in your family. Find a cause to support not only at Christmas but all year long. Revisit those goals on a regular basis.
- To make room for new gifts, have each family member donate a few toys, tools, or clothes to a charity before Christmas.
- Put a visual reminder of goals where your family can see it: a photo of a child you support, the logo of an organization, a chart with lines for marking off specific small goals along the way.

God loves a cheerful giver.

2 CORINTHIANS 9:7 NRSV

A Christmas Gift to God

BY CONNIE DECKER

*Without question, the person who has the power to give
a blessing is greater than the one who is blessed.*

HEBREWS 7:7 NLT

Our family-owned burger place was important to me too, but there were better places to be on Christmas Eve. "Dad, can't we go home? Nobody's going to come to a drive-in on Christmas Eve," I said.

Before Dad could answer, a car drove up. I walked outside to take the couple's order. "Do you still give free dinners to couples on their anniversary?" the young man asked.

"Sure do," I said. This pair looked like they hadn't had a square meal to eat in quite a while.

I brought them their burgers and helped Dad shut down. "Need anything else?" I asked the couple.

"Well, we sure could use a jump," the woman said.

"I have an old battery you can borrow," Dad said. Dad installed it and the couple were off.

Dad and I went back in the drive-in for our coats. "Bundle up," he said. "It'll be a long, cold walk home."

"Don't tell me our car won't start."

"Not without a battery," Dad said. "I gave mine to them!"

It was a long, cold walk home. But Dad and his good deeds kept me warm. There was no place better to be on Christmas Eve than by his side, wherever he was.

God will generously provide all you need.
Then you will always have everything you need and
plenty left over to share with others.

2 CORINTHIANS 9:8 NLT

UNCLE JERRY'S CARAMEL ROLLS

Make these gooey rolls and everyone will want to come to your house for Christmas. There is some brief preparation required the night before, leaving only the baking for a wonderful morning gift for the whole family.

Directions

The night before, melt in a saucepan:

1 cup vanilla ice cream

1 cup brown sugar

1 stick butter

Then pour into the bottom of a 9 x 13-inch cake pan.

Using frozen cinnamon rolls, place 16 rolls, evenly spaced, in cake pan. Cover loosely and leave out overnight.

The next morning, preheat oven to 350 degrees, then bake for 30 minutes. Cool slightly and flip upside down onto platter.

Christmas is doing a little something extra for someone.

CHARLES M. SCHULZ

CHAPTER 7

The simple joy of God's Creation

The more I study nature,
the more I am amazed at the Creator.

LOUIS PASTEUR

Through him all things were made;
without him nothing was made that has been made.

JOHN 1:3 NIV

Jesus, Mary, Joseph, and... Skipper?

BY PEGGY ARCHER

Every creature of God is good.
1 TIMOTHY 4:4 NKJV

We had been saving up all year to buy one of those life-sized Nativity sets that you put up in your front yard—Mary, Joseph, and a Baby Jesus that light up. I also wanted to have a shepherd with sheep or a donkey, but when I counted up the spare change we'd saved in a jar, we had barely enough to buy the trio. Next year it will be less bare, I promised myself.

It snowed the day we put all the figures up. My husband, Chuck, who's handy, hammered together a stable and we set out a bale of straw. The kids played in the yard with Skipper, our little black border-collie mix who seemed most interested in the bale of straw for the manger.

Pretty soon the snow was coming down fast and heavy. I called the kids inside to take their baths while Chuck finished setting up the wiring and then turned the figures on. It was getting dark, so the effect was pretty dramatic. And that's when we noticed: Where was Skipper?

"Skipper!" I called, trudging through our neighbors' yards. Chuck got in the car and drove around the neighborhood. No luck. Poor Skipper, and on such a cold night like this too!

"Let's pray to Baby Jesus," I told the kids when I went back into the house, thinking of the little figure glowing in the manger outside. Just then the phone rang. It was a friend calling to say how much she liked our beautiful new Nativity. "And the dog is such a sweet touch," she added.

Dog? We threw on our coats and boots over pajamas and hurried outside. There, in Chuck's handmade stable, sleeping on the straw at the foot of the manger, was Skipper.

Bare? A manger scene? How could I ever think so.

SUGAR COOKIE ORNAMENTS

Surprise an elderly neighbor or young friend with a miniature tree decorated with delicious sugar cookie ornaments.

Ingredients

- ¾ cup confectioners sugar
- ½ cup butter or margarine, softened
- 1 egg yolk
- 1 teaspoon vanilla extract
- ½ teaspoon almond extract
- 1¼ cup flour
- ½ teaspoon baking soda
- ¼ teaspoon cream of tartar
- 1/8 teaspoon of salt
- Tubes of decorating icing and candy sprinkles
- Nylon string (for hanging)

Directions

In a large mixing bowl, combine sugar, butter, egg yolk, and extracts, beating until fluffy. In another bowl, combine flour, baking soda, cream of tartar, and salt. Stir flour mixture into butter mixture. Wrap dough in plastic wrap. Chill at least two hours.

Preheat oven to 350 degrees. Using a floured rolling pin, roll out dough to 1/8-inch thickness on a floured surface. Cut out cookies (smaller shapes work best), transfer to lightly greased baking sheet. Bake 5 to 7 minutes or until very lightly browned. While cookies are warm, use a toothpick to make a hole for hanging. Transfer to wire rack for cooling. Once cooled, decorate with colorful icing and candy accents. Let air dry until icing hardens. Makes about five dozen.

A Christmas Wind

BY PEGGY FREZON

I call on you, O God, for you will answer me....
Show me the wonders of your great love.

PSALM 17:6–7 NIV

Our new, artificial Christmas tree was more convenient than a real one. That's what I told myself as I helped my husband, Mike, set it up. It was less expensive. It came in three easy pieces that opened out like umbrellas. The branches were pre-wrapped with tiny white bulbs. No pine needles to vacuum, no water tray to refill. So why was I unsatisfied?

"It's not the same," I said as Mike and I finished. "A real tree is a bit of nature brought inside."

"But it looks great," Mike said. "Perfect, in fact." We'd chosen the tallest model in the store. The branches brushed right up against the ceiling. "It'll look even better when we get our old ornaments on it."

I opened the storage boxes while Mike strung extra lights. One by one we hung our familiar decorations from years past. The pipe cleaner reindeer Andy made in second grade. His sister Kate's snowflake covered in blue glue glitter. The kids were grown and on their own now. They wouldn't miss the piney smell of a real tree in our living room. But I did. The bayberry and pine candles I'd lit on the windowsill just weren't doing the trick.

The tree was finished—except for one thing. The star at the top. *Maybe that will turn this into a real Christmas tree*, I thought as I took our topper out of the box.

I climbed up on the stepladder and reached into the branches. "Mike!" I said. "It won't fit! The tree's too tall."

"That's one advantage to a real tree," Mike admitted. "You can lop off the top." We stood there frowning, wondering what to do.

"I could hang it," I said. Mike threaded some wire through the star and I climbed back up the ladder to hook it on. The tree top sank under its weight. The tip of our extra-large pine flopped over like the scraggly tree from *A Charlie Brown Christmas*.

"Maybe I can find something at the mall," I said, putting the old star away. The tree top looked bare—and artificial—without it. All the nice tree toppers were sure to be gone by now.

That night I lay in bed listening to the blustery wind and blowing outside. *God, you know how much I love to have a star on my tree. Help me find something.* Wind rattled the windows. Otherwise God was silent.

The next morning I went outside to get the paper. Evidence of the windstorm was everywhere. Twigs, sticks and branches littered the lawn. Our driveway was full of pinecones from a tree all the way up the block. As I leaned down to pick up the paper, my eye fell on a pile of twigs lying on the ground. *They look almost like a star*, I thought, my mind going back to my Christmas tree. I looked at the branches again. Had the wind really made that pattern all on its own? I had an idea. I grabbed some branches and a handful of those cones from the neighbor's tree. I took everything inside and got out my glue gun. At the kitchen table I arranged and rearranged them in a star pattern until I got it just right. I didn't even look up when Mike said bye before he left for work. "Don't look," I said. "It's a surprise."

I glued the branches in place and added pinecones for decoration and tied a raffia bow at the bottom. By the time Mike got home from work, our new lightweight Christmas star was hanging proudly at the top of our tree, filling the room with the familiar smell of wood and pine I'd missed so much.

A bit of nature—and a bit of heavenly inspiration—had made our artificial convenience a real Christmas tree after all. Never again would I hear the wind blow and think God was being silent.

TIPS FOR CRAFTING WITH KIDS

Creating Christmas crafts using things from nature is especially appropriate during the holidays. Gathering pinecones, feathers, branches, nests, and other things to make beautiful wreaths, centerpieces, and art projects is a fun way to celebrate God's amazing creativity. Here's some tips to make it less work and more fun.

- Crafts can be messy, chose a workspace that is easy to clean, well lit, and ventilated.
- Use waxed paper or a drop cloth to cover work surface. Keep paper towels and a damp sponge on hand for spills or sticky fingers.
- Read the instructions to the end before beginning, have little ones help bring materials to the work space.
- Go over any safety precautions. Explain that some tools can be dangerous and are used only by adults.
- Let younger kids work at their own skill level and speed. Remember, the memory is in the doing. The best results are usually a bit crooked and colored in the "wrong" spots.

I remember the whole reason for Christmas—
Jesus Christ! The gift of God is eternal life.
What generosity! What love!
I'm thankful to the giver of all.
I'm thankful for Christmas.

LINDA R. WADE

How easy it would be for the shepherd to find Him.
No other newly born babe would be found
"lying in a manger"—just One—and He,
the altogether lovely One,
the chiefest among ten thousand!

CHARLES HURLBURT AND T. C. HORTON

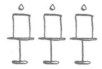

HOLIDAY FIRE STARTERS

The weather outside may be frightful, but the fire can be delightful much quicker with these scented pinecone fire starters. Let the kids help, but just be sure to keep a careful eye on those sweet young ones around the hot wax.

You will need:
Pinecones, paraffin, a double boiler or electric frying pan, a can to melt paraffin in, tongs, red crayons with paper removed (for coloring wax), cinnamon oil (1 teaspoon per 1 ½ pounds of paraffin), and newspaper.

Cover work area with newspaper. Melt paraffin in double broiler over hot water or in a can in an electric frying pan filled with water. *Do not melt paraffin over an open flame or directly on burner.* Add pieces of red crayon to melted paraffin. Add cinnamon oil.

With tongs, dip pinecones in wax. Repeat for several coats, allowing paraffin to dry on sheets of wax paper between coats. Allow to dry completely before using.

To use, simply place several pinecones under logs and light cones. Creates a light, pleasing aroma, and adds a decorative touch in a basket near the fireplace or as a centerpiece.

It is good to be children sometimes,
and never better than at Christmas,
when its mighty Founder was a child Himself.

CHARLES DICKENS

Jesus called for them saying,
"Permit the children to come to Me,
and do not hinder them,
for the kingdom of God belongs
to such as these."

LUKE 18:16 NASB

CHAPTER 8

The simple joy of

Christmas Memories

Our hearts grow tender with childhood memories
and love of kindred, and we are better throughout
the year for having, in spirit, become a child
again at Christmas-time.

LAURA INGALLS WILDER

Children are a gift from the LORD;
they are a reward from him.

PSALM 127:3 NLT

A Gift to Remember

BY BARBARA FELTS BESS

Man looks at the outward appearance, but the Lord looks at the heart.
1 SAMUAL 16:7 NKJV

One Michigan Christmas nearly fifty years ago will stay with me for the rest of my life.

Snow covered the ground in a blanket of white. Excitement was in the air. In my second-grade class, there was a buzz about the party and exchange of gifts.

We had been making preparations for weeks. There were handmade snowflakes tacked to the walls and stars hanging from the ceiling. Red and green garlands looped across the top of the blackboard.

My class was the usual mix of kids, but one stood out. Her name was Kristy. She came to school in frayed dresses and run-down shoes. Her hair was never combed all the way, and we often noticed dirt on her legs. "Doesn't she take a bath?" we whispered. But Kristy didn't make excuses about her appearance. She was always friendly. She seemed completely accepting of herself.

Each of us brought a gift to the Christmas party. Boys gave to boys, girls to girls. We put our gifts on the wide ledge of our room's bay windows. One gift stood out. It was cylindrical. The paper was ripped at one end and the narrow ribbon was frayed. Kristy noticed my horrified expression. "It's a good present," she insisted. "The wrapping's torn, that's all."

After lunch and recess we trooped back to our room, eager for the festivities. We squirmed in our seats as our teacher walked up and down the rows. She held two hats. One contained numbers for the boys, the other for us girls. The teacher had put corresponding numbers on the presents.

When my turn came I reached into the hat. Many beautifully wrapped gifts still lay on the window ledge. I drew a number, then went to match it at the window ledge. "Oh, no," I sighed. It was Kristy's gift. My classmates clucked.

"I think you'll like it," Kristy said.

At last all the packages had been claimed. Our teacher said it was time to open them. I felt Kristy's eyes on me. I just knew it was a terrible gift. But what would I say? I didn't want to hurt Kristy's feelings.

I couldn't have been more surprised. Inside, rolled into a cylinder, were two of my favorite things in the whole world: a coloring book and a dot-to-dot. I looked at Kristy. "This is a very good present," I said. "Thank you." Kristy grinned. For once I didn't see her old clothes and messy hair. I saw a friendly girl who had given me the perfect gift.

I don't remember anything else I received that Christmas. My family moved away the next year, and I never saw Kristy again. We hadn't become best friends, but I reached an understanding because of her. The outside of a person, or the wrapping on a gift, isn't what's important. It's what's inside that counts.

Celebration is more than a happy feeling.
Celebration is an experience.
It is liking others, accepting others,
laughing with others.

DOUGLAS R. STUVA

*J*ust a few short years from now our children and families will look back on this holiday season. What will they remember? What emotions and nostalgia will your family traditions incite?… This year we can make the decision that despite chaos and distractions of the season, it's our family and relationships that matter most…. Kids will not remember what video game or gadget they were playing or the movie that they were watching on DVD (unless, that is, you're doing it together and that becomes your tradition).They will remember time spent together and the interaction of a loving family gathering.

SHIRLEY DOBSON

Memories are perhaps the best gifts of all.

GLORIA GAITHER

12 DAYS OF CHRISTMAS TOGETHERNESS

Create memories that will last a lifetime.

Day 1: Check your local paper for holiday events. Most cities have concerts or plays that could become traditional (and influence a future musician or actor in the family). If attending a concert, ask your children if they can pick out the sound of each instrument. Then on the way home, ask them how an orchestra is like a family.

Day 2: Take an after-dark drive without personal electronic devices: turn on a favorite Christmas CD or playlist in the car and enjoy family conversation as you enjoy the brightly lit houses in your neighborhood or beyond.

Day 3: Have a family Christmas movie marathon night with a trivia question for the kids before the movie starts. (For example, what object does George Bailey get frustrated with and want to throw, but later ends up kissing in *It's A Wonderful Life*?)

Day 4: Volunteer at your local senior citizens center or nursing home, bringing cookies or homemade crafts made by your children. Sometimes just seeing those young ones will put a smile on the residents' faces and bring back cherished memories.

Day 5: Play a card or board game. Have a contest to see who can be the most creatively over-the-top encourager to one another.

Day 6: Camp out in the living room in front of the Christmas tree.

Day 7: Cook a holiday recipe as a family.

Day 8: Make puppets by sewing buttons and drawing with markers on old socks. Put on a puppet show using the couch to hide the humans.

Day 9: Roast marshmallows over a campfire or in the fireplace.

Day 10: String popcorn and cranberries for a tree in the yard.

Day 11: Go caroling together, door to door or at a nursing home. Have children bring their musical instruments if they have them.

Day 12: Invite family, friends, and neighbors over on a December evening for games, dessert, and reading of the Christmas story in Luke 2:1–20.

Children learn they are valued when we spend time with them.
It will increase joy and instill confidence in them as they grow,
while making memories they'll keep for a lifetime.

BONNIE JENSEN

*Truly I tell you, whatever you did for one
of the least of these. . .you did for me.*

MATTHEW 25:40 NIV

Empty Nest Christmas

BY PEGGY FREZON

Jesus Christ is the same yesterday and today and forever.

HEBREWS 13:8 NIV

My husband, Mike, emerged from the basement, lugging a dusty, bulky box—ornaments for our eight-foot Fraser fir. "That should do it," said Mike, lowering the box with a grunt. Just the sight of them should have made me happy. I love Christmas. But this year it just didn't seem the same.

A few days before, our daughter, Kate, had called to say she'd be spending Christmas with her fiancé Aaron's family in North Carolina. They had met a year earlier at Cornell, where Kate was a senior. I was thrilled for her. But now I realized—she wouldn't be decorating this tree. Or opening presents Christmas morning. Or eating Christmas dinner. By next year she'd be graduated and married, living who knows where.

Clattering sounded above, and my sixteen-year-old, Andy, bounded down the stairs. "Just in time to decorate!" I called to him, smiling.

"Sorry, Mom, gotta go. Guys are waiting!" He rushed out the door, basketball in hand.

I turned to Mike, but he was bent under the tree, pouring water in the stand.

I remembered just one year earlier, when Kate was home from school and all four of us had listened to Bing Crosby carols while covering the tree with ornaments. I had marveled then at how effortlessly Andy stood on a stool and reached atop the tree. He was six feet tall! How had that happened?

"You know what?" said Mike, working his way out from under the tree. "I think I might have missed a box. I'll go check." He trooped down to the basement, and I turned to the big box on the floor. We'd collected a lot of ornaments in twenty-six years of marriage. I pulled out a delicate blown glass star and hung it from a branch. The branch drooped. *I know how you feel*, I thought and sat in a chair.

Mike returned from the basement with another especially dusty, slightly battered box.

"Let's finish tomorrow," I said, silently projecting ahead to next year, when Andy, too, would be away at college. "I think I'm done with Christmas for today."

That night, turning restlessly in bed, I shared my troubles with the Lord. *I know what the true joy of the season is—your birth. But I feel like my family is slipping away.*

The next morning Mike and I tackled the boxes. What was in that old one, anyway? I didn't recognize it. I blew a layer of dust away and pried it open. Yellowed tissue paper crinkled. I reached in and pulled out something rough, a construction-paper star, about the size of my hand, covered in sparkly glitter. I gasped. Nearly twenty years before, Kate had come home from preschool and proudly presented us with that star. I could still see the glitter covering her hands.

I reached in again, and out came a Styrofoam ball, blobbed with glue, beads, and more glitter. "Mike, look!" I said. Mike knelt beside me and we both grinned at Andy's trademark handiwork with a bottle of Elmer's®. The box yielded more treasures: a crooked paper chain connected with dozens of staples. A popsicle-stick reindeer with a red poof-ball nose. An empty pudding container filled with confetti, Polaroids of the kids glued to cardboard circles and threaded with yarn.

Shoving the other boxes aside, we went to work. My spirits rose with each one—each tiny Christmas memory, all those mornings when Kate and Andy would perch at the top of the stairs, Santa hats crooked on their heads, waiting for Mom and Dad to arrange the last gifts and light the tree before coming down.

Okay, Lord. So they're growing up, moving on. That's good, right? I slipped an arm around Mike's waist and looked at the tree. Christmas would change—our family would change. Andy would soon head off to college, and maybe one day we'd be having Christmas at Kate and Aaron's house, putting up ornaments their kids had made. *Memories aren't just about the past, are they, Lord? They're your way of reassuring us you'll be there in the future too.* What a wonderful gift

That evening Kate called from North Carolina. "I miss you guys!" she said. "I'm having a great time here, but I wish I could be there with you."

"Funny you should say that, sweetheart," I said. "You'll never guess what we found in an old box...."

Christmas tree baubles only become valuable when they are veterans.

PETER GRAY

MAKING MEMORIES CORN SALSA

This is a great recipe to make together with friends or family. After it is complete, give each participant a jar of salsa to take home to help keep the memories alive.

Ingredients
Heat over medium heat until dissolved:
   2 tablespoon olive oil
   ½ cup cider vinegar
   ¼ cup sugar

Combine in large bowl:
   1 yellow pepper, diced
   1 red pepper, diced
   1 green pepper, diced
   2-4 stalks celery, diced
   ½ cup red onion, diced
   2 cups frozen corn, thawed
   15 oz. can pinto beans, drained and rinsed
   15 oz. can black beans, drained and rinsed

Directions
Pour vinegar mixture over and mix well. Marinate overnight. Pour off excess liquid and serve with tortilla chips.

   Add or substitute what you have on hand, such as black-eyed peas, kidney beans, zucchini, avocados, black olives, radishes, pimentos, garlic, cilantro, etc.

   Fill small jars with salsa to give as gifts. Keep refrigerated.

We light a thousand candles bright
around the earth today,
And all the beams will shine
across the heaven's grand display.
Dear brightest star o'er Bethlehem,
O let your precious light
Shine in with hope and peace toward men
In every home tonight.

SWEDISH CAROL
(TRANSLATION BY EVIE KARLSSON TORNQUIST)

For God in all his fullness was pleased to live in Christ,
and through him God reconciled everything to himself.

COLOSSIANS 1:19–20 NLT

SIMPLE WAYS TO TELL CHILDREN "I LOVE YOU"

During the Christmas season, time seems to speed up, robbing parents and grandparents of quality time with their kids. Here are some tips for letting them know they are still special.

- Spend time shopping with each child alone. Put the date on the family calendar so everyone can see it and anticipate it.

- Let your children overhear you compliment them for the gifts God has given to them, such as the gift of kindness, encouragement, generosity, etc.

- Celebrate everyday simple accomplishments, like wrapping a present themselves, or just being a good helper by putting a finger on the ribbon to keep it in place while tying.

- Pray with them and tell God how wonderful it is being their parent or grandparent.

- Don't allow other things to distract you when they want to talk. Really listen. The gifts that need to be wrapped can wait.

- Teach children to do something you loved doing as a child at Christmas. Or choose something new to learn together.

- Proudly wear the jewelry and display the artwork or object they have given you.

- Amid the hustle of the holiday, make the effort to eat dinner together as often as possible. Use the time to let them know how thankful you are for family time.

CHAPTER 9

The simple joy of
Christmas Wonder

Whether sixty or sixteen, there is in every human being's heart
the love of wonder, the sweet amazement at the stars and star-like
things, the undaunted challenge of events, the unfailing childlike
appetite for what-next, and the joy of the game of living.

SAMUEL ULLMAN

*The star they had seen when it rose went ahead of them
until it stopped over the place where the child was.
When they saw the star, they were overjoyed.*

MATTHEW 2:9–10 NIV

Making Christmas

BY BROCK KIDD

A new spirit will I put within you.

EZEKIEL 36:26 KJV

*C*hristmas was creeping up on me and I was so busy basking in the year's successes that I hadn't given the holiday much thought. I tallied up my clients' gains and muttered "Well done" under my breath as I shut down my computer.

That night I had dinner with some associates. "This is what it's all about," I said as I made a toast to the group. Everyone nodded in agreement.

The next day was Christmas Eve, and being the quintessential last-minute shopper, I headed to the mall. Carols were blaring through the speakers as people bustled about, but I felt empty.

The next morning I pulled up behind the line of cars parked on my parents' street. Every year my family hosts a Christmas brunch, mostly for people who have no family or no place to go. *Why can't we just have our own Christmas?* I thought as I walked through the front door. I breathed in the smell of country ham and baking biscuits. Kate, who had never missed one of these gatherings, was leaning on her walker near the fireplace, watching my niece Abby playing with her new doll. In the kitchen my mother was laughing as she dished out the cheese grits.

I recognized it first on the faces of the people gathered around her. It spread through the house and finally it filled up my heart—the spirit of Christmas, the biggest dividend of all. And in that moment I understood that investing *in* people is a lot more important than investing *for* them.

*Christmas is the season for
kindling the fire of hospitality in the hall,
the genial flame of charity in the heart.*

WASHINGTON IRVING

If a child is to keep his inborn sense of wonder...he needs
the companionship of at least one adult who can share it,
rediscovering with him the joy, excitement,
and mystery of the world we live in.

RACHEL CARSON

Life holds no sweeter thing than this—
To teach a little child the tale most loved on earth
And watch the wonder deepen in his eyes
The while you tell him of the Christ Child's birth;
The while you tell of shepherds and a song,
Of gentle drowsy beasts and fragrant hay
On which that starlit night in Bethlehem
God's tiny Son and his young mother lay.

ADELAIDE LOVE

She brought forth her firstborn son,
and wrapped him in swaddling clothes,
and laid him in a manger;
because there was no room for them in the inn.

LUKE 2:7 KJV

Standing on the Promises

BY TED NACE

Let us hold unswervingly to the hope we profess,
for he who promised is faithful.

HEBREWS 10:23 NIV

Christmas has always been a particularly poignant time for my wife Kathy and me. Our first child Ryan was born the week before Christmas with a rare disorder that caused massive internal bleeding.

The neonatal intensive care staff encouraged us to baptize our perfectly formed, yet incredibly ill baby, and we did, with a cross of iron nails on the shelf above his bassinet as our visual claim of God's promises.

Then, on Christmas Eve, the nurse in charge pulled two rocking chairs close to Ryan's bed. She stretched out all of his tubing and monitor wires so that Kathy and I could hold him for the first time since his birth. It was the most wonderful Christmas gift we had ever been given.

Now fast-forward thirty-one years: this miracle baby is now our pastor. Kathy and I are snuggled together in a pew at St. John's Church in Red Hook, New York, surrounded by Alicia, our son Kyle's fiancée, and our son Joel and his wife Alyssa, their newborn son Conner cradled in their arms. Tonight, Kyle is playing Joseph. He walks slowly down the center aisle, tenderly holding the elbow of Mary, portrayed by Ryan's wife Jennifer. In her arms, wrapped in white bunting, is their baby Austin as the Christ Child. The church is bathed in candlelight as Ryan's expressive voice retells the story of Christmas. When Ryan sees this Holy Family—his family—approaching him, tears spill down his face—and mine.

This is the irrational season
When love blossoms bright and wild.
Had Mary been filled with reason
There'd have been no room for the child.
MADELEINE L'ENGLE

To be grateful is to recognize the love of God in everything
He has given us—and He has given us everything. Every breath we draw
is a gift of His love, every moment of existence is a gift of grace.
THOMAS MERTON

You can revive your sense of wonder by merely saying to yourself: Suppose this were the only time. Suppose this sunset, this moonrise, this symphony, this buttered toast, this sleeping child, this flag against the sky…suppose you would never experience these things again! Few things are commonplace in themselves. It's our reaction to them that grows dull, as we move forward through the years.

ARTHUR GORDON

Out of his fullness we have all received grace in place of grace already given.

JOHN 1:16 NIV

I call on you, O God, for you will answer me;
turn your ear to me and hear my prayer.
Show the wonder of your great love.

PSALM 17:6–7 NIV

A Savior in the Straw

BY DANIEL SCHANTZ

The firstborn of the poor will feed,
and the needy will lie down in safety.

ISAIAH 14:30 NKJV

I've heard that America's favorite Christmas carol is "Away in a Manger." Little wonder! To think that a simple wooden box filled with hay was all God needed to incubate the Savior of the world!

To me, the message of the manger is simplicity. The Son of God Himself was delivered without health insurance, anesthesia, antibiotics, LPNs or MDs. I have been to many Christmas pageants, and every year they seem to get more affluent and elaborate.

The Christmas program that is forever burned in my heart is the one that took place in our living room when I was a boy. The six of us kids sat 'round the tree, singing "Silent Night," while Mom and Dad snuggled on the couch. My handsome father slowly read the Christmas story in his rich baritone voice and ended with a prayer of thanks for Jesus. Then we exchanged gifts.

Christmas doesn't get any better than that.

Come now with joy to worship and adore him;
hushed in the stillness, wonder and behold
Christ in the stable where his mother bore him,
Christ whom the prophets faithfully foretold.

TIMOTHY DUDLEY-SMITH

Behold, the virgin shall be with child and shall bear a Son,
and they shall call His name Immanuel,
which translated means "GOD with us."

MATTHEW 1:23 NASB

Timeless this moment when God becomes man,
So timeless the world will remember,
This birth means our waiting has come to an end,
And now is a new beginning....
Into time has come the Timeless One.

KEN PARKER

Delivering Christmas Love

BY DAN SHORT

We have different gifts, according to the grace given to each of us.
ROMANS 12:6 NIV

By my age I always imagined I'd be on the verge of retirement, comfortable with who I was. I was neither. The company I'd helped build from the ground up had just laid me off. At age fifty-seven I had no job, a balding head of white hair, and a bulging stomach. What could life possibly have in store for me at this late stage in the game?

One December afternoon I scanned the want ads. But nothing ever seemed right for me. More to the point, I didn't seem right for anything.

"I'm going to do some Christmas shopping at the mall," my wife said. "Want to join me?" Happy for the distraction, I went along. I waited on a bench in the central court. Little children skipped by with their parents, and my mind drifted back to Christmases when my own kids were small.

I got up from the bench to stretch. Somehow I hadn't noticed the ornately carved chair. Santa sat in it, large as life. He looked into the child's eyes and spoke softly. The child broke into a huge grin. That's just the way Santa should be, I thought. He radiated a love and gentleness that made him the perfect symbol of Christmas, when God gave the world the gift of His love in a humble manger.

I started finding reasons to go to the mall on my own. I would plant myself with a view of Santa and the children. A few days before Christmas, I went again. I watched Santa for a while, until he stood to take a break. To my surprise, he headed over to talk to me!

I held out my hand. "I love watching you work, Santa," I blurted out.

"I've noticed," he said, shaking my hand in a firm grip.

"I hope I haven't disturbed you." His blue eyes twinkled.

"Ever thought about being Santa?" he said. "You seem like a natural." Me? A natural?

He patted my shoulder and handed me a slip of paper. "Give me a call after Christmas," he said.

Right after the first of the year I called the number. It turned out Naturally Santa, Inc. was an elite group of men. In order to be accepted I had to audition in front of an entire roomful of Santas! Later I got a call from Billy Gootch, the founder.

"We want you to be one of us," he said.

In September I attended Santa School. I eagerly gathered tips and kept careful notes. One day I asked an experienced Santa, "What do you do if a child asks for something you can't give him?"

"That happens all the time," he said. "I think it's best to be honest…. I also keep a supply of sleigh bells. One of those lets a child know he's special, no matter what."

By the time December rolled around I was eager to start—but also nervous.

A few days into the job a little boy with big brown eyes climbed onto my knee. I took his hands.

"What's your name?" I asked softly.

"Kevin," he replied.

"And what would you like Santa to bring you for Christmas, Kevin?"

Kevin looked down at the ground. "I want my mommy back." My heart pounded as Kevin explained that his mother had left him and his father. "For good this time, I think," the boy said.

"Santa's a toy maker, Kevin. He can't fix your problem. Only God can. But I'll pray for the three of you." I pulled out a sleigh bell on a leather string and tied it gently around Kevin's wrist. "I only give a reindeer bracelet like this to a few special children."

Kevin gave the bell a shake. "Really?" he said, perking up. I knew what I heard in his voice: hope.

"Life has many good things in store for you, Kevin. I can see your Dad loves you very much." The boy nodded. "And do you know what? Santa loves you too."

Kevin hugged me around my neck and skipped over to his dad's open arms.

God loves Kevin too, I thought. So much so that he put him on the lap of the very Santa who understood perhaps better than any other. Life had great things in store since I'd found the job of delivering Christmas love, to one child at a time.

As we grow in our capacities to
see and enjoy the joys that God
has placed in our lives, life
becomes a glorious experience of
discovering His endless wonders.

WENDY MOORE

The wonder of our Lord is that He is so accessible to us in the common things of our lives: the cup of water...breaking of the bread...welcoming children into our arms...fellowship over a meal... giving thanks. A simple attitude of caring, listening, and lovingly telling the truth.

NANCIE CARMICHAEL

God moves in a mysterious way
His wonders to perform;
He plants His footsteps in the sea,
And rides upon the storm.

WILLIAM COWPER

I look behind me and you're there, then up ahead and you're there, too—your reassuring presence, coming and going. This is too much, too wonderful—I can't take it all in!

PSALM 139:5–6 MSG

CHAPTER 10

The simple joy of Christmas All Year

My idea of Christmas, whether old-fashioned or modern,
is very simple: loving others. Come to think of it,
why do we have to wait for Christmas to do that?

BOB HOPE

I thank my God always, making mention of you in my prayers,
because I hear of your love and of the faith
which you have toward the Lord Jesus.

PHILEMON 1:4–5

Christmas in June

BY KAREN M. LEET

Each of you should use whatever gift you have received to serve others, as faithful stewards of God's grace in its various forms.

1 PETER 4:10 NIV

One year my parents, retired and living in Florida, decided to stop exchanging Christmas gifts. Instead, they'd give to their favorite charities, using the money they would have spent on each other: dog food for the Humane Society, canned goods to a homeless shelter, toys to Toys for Tots.

Delighted with their new gift strategy, Mom decided on a year-long project. She'd buy dolls on sale—Barbies and other kinds—and clothes for them too. Then a few weeks before Christmas she'd assemble kits with a doll, at least five new outfits, accessories, and even her own handmade hats and tote bags, and donate them to a worthy organization. Her idea became a family tradition. I joined the project and so did my daughter.

Mom died last year, but her project lives on as our family stockpiles dolls and outfits for next Christmas. It's fun to do a little Christmas shopping all year—even in the summertime. And I smile, remembering Mom's delight in her dolls and her pleasure in giving joy to others.

Christmas is a time of the heart,
not just a date. Its meaning transcends time.
Jesus was born to love us and fill our lives
with Himself.

If there is love in your heart, Christmas can last forever.

MARION SCHOEBERLEIN

Whoever regards one day as special does so to the Lord.

ROMANS 14:6 NIV

CHRISTMAS (PRAYER) CARDS

I have not stopped giving thanks for you,
remembering you in my prayers.

EPHESIANS 1:16 NIV

Isn't it like getting Christmas gifts early when we receive Christmas cards from loved ones in the mail, our name in their handwriting? We love hearing how friends and family are doing—especially if they're far away. Here are a few suggestions that have worked for others, to keep those loved ones in our prayers while holding onto a little bit of Christmas spirit year 'round.

- Jackie in Wisconsin saves the Christmas cards she receives in a stylish tin next to her favorite chair. She takes a few cards out each week for her morning devotions and includes them in her prayers.

- Susan of New York says that her mother takes one Christmas card out a day, prays for the person who sent it, then writes a letter letting her friend know she's praying for them.

- Jayne, from South Carolina, also jots a note or makes a quick call to her friends, just so that they know how important they are to her.

What if Christmas day were both a beginning and an end?
The beginning of a celebration of Jesus that would not end
until the next Christmas, when it would begin all over again?

MICHAEL CARD

The faithful love of the Lord never ends!
His mercies never cease
Great is his faithfulness;
His mercies begin afresh each morning.

LAMENTATIONS 3:22–23 NLT

Men and women everywhere sigh on December 26
and say they're glad Christmas is all over for another year.
But it isn't over. "Unto you is born...a Savior." It's just beginning!
And it will go on forever.

EUGENIA PRICE

Christmas in April

BY ALEXIS HURD-SHIRES

They who seek the LORD shall not be in want of any good thing.

PSALM 34:10 NASB

*T*he shelves in the orphanage pantry were almost bare. I'd been volunteering for months at this Romanian orphanage and always marveled at how we'd survived, but our supplies had never been this low. Twenty kids to feed with just a little pasta.

Unexpected bills had exhausted our funds. I'd sent a request to my church back in Oklahoma at Christmastime and they'd been generous. We'd also had help from a German relief agency and their leader Rosa, who normally visited in December.

But all the food they'd given us had run out, and I was running out of hope.

I went up to my room and turned on the computer. I'd send another appeal to my church. But even with e-mail, I feared their gifts wouldn't reach us in time. *Dear God, we need something now.*

Later that evening I was in my room when someone knocked on my door. "What is it?" I asked. "Rosa's here!" one of the children shouted. Rosa? I wondered. She only comes in December. I ran down the stairs.

"We're here in Romania to interview a new employee," she said. "We thought we'd drop by to see how you're doing. I hope this isn't a bad time. Is there anything you need?" Bad time? I thought. Perfect time! I hopped in her van and we went to the market. We returned with rice, beans, sugar, jelly, a box of bananas—everything we needed, and then some.

That night as I climbed into bed, a passage from Isaiah came to mind: "Before they call, I will answer, and while they are yet speaking, I will hear" (Isaiah 65:24). And indeed God had.

The joy of brightening other lives, bearing each other's burdens, easing other's loads, and supplanting empty hearts and lives with generous gifts becomes for us the magic of Christmas.

W. C. JONES

What can I give him, poor as I am?
If I were a shepherd, I would give him a lamb,
If I were a Wise Man, I would do my part,
But what I can I give him, give my heart.

CHRISTINA ROSSETTI

What keeps the wild hope of Christmas alive year after year in a
world notorious for dashing all hopes is the haunting dream that
the child who was born that day may yet be born again even in us
and our own snowbound, snowblind longing for Him.

FREDERICK BUECHNER

One thing I ask from the LORD,
this only do I seek:
that I may dwell in the
house of the LORD
all the days of my life.

PSALM 27:4 NIV

All That Glitters

BY PENNY MUSCO

God is love. Whoever lives in love lives in God, and God in them.

1 JOHN 4:16 NIV

You date a man for three months. After a year you marry him. By your first Christmas together as wife and husband, you think you know everything about him.

And then you go shopping together for Christmas decorations.

That first year together, Joe and I picked out the perfect tree. We found some boxes of old-fashioned ornaments that reminded me of my family's decorations. Walking down an aisle I spotted a tinsel display. I reached for a box.

"No." Joe said, guiding my hands away from the box. "No tinsel."

"What?" I asked him. "No tinsel?" I gave him a quizzical look, trying not to look as shocked as I felt.

"I'm not wild about it," he said. "Never have been."

I argued. I kept at him for a week. At last he relented—on one condition.

"We'll buy one box and that's it—forever. You'll have to take it off the tree and reuse it." This is the man I married? Maybe he was crazy.

Still, I had married Joe for better or for worse and this was the only negative. I figured I would decorate the tree with tinsel, and once he saw how lovely it looked, he would change his mind.

Almost a quarter century went by and nothing changed. Until last Christmas. I unearthed the box of used tinsel from the attic. The life expectancy of a strand, I've learned, is only about one year. I showed the depleted box, its red and green now faded and dull, to Joe.

Joe got a stubborn look in his eyes. "No," he said. This was the only blip in our wonderful marriage. But twenty-five tinsel-deprived years was enough. *Next year I'll buy a fresh box,* I thought, *and sneak in some new strands—few enough so he won't turn suspicious.*

Instead of buying each other gifts for our anniversary, Joe and I decided to throw a party for ourselves. A few nights before the party, we sat on the couch and snuggled. I felt so close to him at that moment, so grateful for all of our wonderful years together, that I experienced a pang of guilt about my plan.

All at once Joe slipped his arm from around my shoulder and pulled a gift-wrapped box from behind him.

"I thought we weren't going to buy each other presents this year," I protested. "I don't have anything for you!"

 "It's for us," he said. I fumbled with the wrapping. Slowly I pulled the lid off the box. Then I started to cry. Inside lay a glistening heap of tinsel—silver, for our silver anniversary.

"Do you know how hard it is to find that stuff in May?" he asked, a smile creeping up the corners of his mouth. "I had to go on the Internet!" I threw my arms around him and held him for what seemed like…twenty-five years.

Later, I let the tinsel spill through my fingers. No, I thought, Joe still isn't crazy about tinsel, but he is crazy about me, and said a prayer of thanks for the gift of my husband.

What happens when we live God's way?
He brings gifts into our lives…
things like affection for others,
exuberance about life, serenity.

GALATIANS 5:22 MSG

Like God, Christmas is timeless and eternal, from everlasting to everlasting. It is something even more than what happened that night in starlit little Bethlehem; it has been behind the stars forever. There was Christmas in the heart of God before the world was formed.

ROY ROGERS

When they saw the star,
they were overjoyed.

MATTHEW 2:10 NIV

[May] you be blessed with joys deeper than any sadness, gratitude happier than any regrets, hopes brighter than the shadows of any discouragement, and the vitality to make of every day what God on Christmas Day made for all days.

LEW SMEDES

ACKNOWLEDGMENTS

"Chain Reaction" by Cheryl Lagler is reprinted with permission from *Guideposts* magazine. Copyright © 2008 by Guideposts. All rights reserved. "Angel of Nuremberg" by Jenny Woolf is reprinted with permission from *Angels on Earth* magazine. Copyright © 2007 by Guideposts. All rights reserved. "A Bob Hope Christmas" by Linda Neukrug is reprinted with permission from *Daily Guideposts*. Copyright © 2006 by Guideposts. All rights reserved. "Christmas Will Find You" by Debra S. Behnke is reprinted with permission from *Angels on Earth* magazine. Copyright © 2008 by Guideposts. All rights reserved. "Always Watching" by Anita Hicks is reprinted with permission from *Angels on Earth* magazine. Copyright © 2010 by Guideposts. All rights reserved. "Not Such a Silent Night" by Vicki Powell is reprinted with permission from *Angels on Earth* magazine. Copyright © 2006 by Guideposts. All rights reserved. "Christmas Magic" by Kitty McCaffrey is reprinted with permission from *Angels on Earth* magazine. Copyright © 2007 by Guideposts. All rights reserved. "Surprised by the Light" by Cathy Wallace is reprinted with permission from *Angels on Earth* magazine. Copyright © 2008 by Guideposts. All rights reserved. "Something to Believe In" by Anne Benedict is reprinted with permission from *Angels on Earth* magazine. Copyright © 2008 by Guideposts. All rights reserved. "A Hidden Glory" by Gail Thorell Schilling is reprinted with permission from *Daily Guideposts*. Copyright © 2006 by Guideposts. All rights reserved. "My Christmas Star" by Frances McGee-Cromartie is reprinted with permission from *Guideposts* magazine. Copyright © 2010 by Guideposts. All rights reserved. "Room at the Inn?" by Linda Breeden is reprinted with permission from *Angels on Earth* magazine. Copyright © 2008 by Guideposts. All rights reserved. "Friendly Skies" by Linda Passarelli is reprinted with permission from *Angels on Earth* magazine. Copyright © 2007 by Guideposts. All rights reserved. "The Night of the Christmas Nurse" written by Karen Tracy is reprinted with permission from *Angels on Earth* magazine. Copyright © 2010 by Guideposts. All rights reserved. "Guide in the Storm" by Lyn Thompson is reprinted with permission from *Angels on Earth* magazine. Copyright © 2008 by Guide-